Archibald Hastie Dick

Outlines of Political Economy

Archibald Hastie Dick

Outlines of Political Economy

ISBN/EAN: 9783744643627

Printed in Europe, USA, Canada, Australia, Japan

Cover: Foto ©Suzi / pixelio.de

More available books at **www.hansebooks.com**

William Collins, Sons, & Co.'s Educational Works.

COLLINS' SCHOOL SERIES.

NEW CODE PROGRESSIVE READERS:
AN ENTIRELY NEW SERIES OF READING BOOKS,
Edited by CANON RIDGWAY, Training College, Culham.
Illustrated by DALZIEL BROTHERS.

Specially adapted to meet the requirements of the New Code.

	S.	D.
FIRST PRIMER, 32 pp., Fcap. 8vo, sewed, 1d; cloth, ...	0	2
SECOND PRIMER, 64 pp., Fcap. 8vo, sewed, 2d; cloth, ...	0	3
FIRST STANDARD, 90 pp., Fcap. 8vo, flush, 4d; cloth,	0	5
SECOND STANDARD, 124 pp., Fcap. 8vo, flush, 6d; cloth,	0	7
THIRD STANDARD, 174 pp., Ex. Fcap. 8vo, cloth, ...	0	9
FOURTH STANDARD, 208 pp., Ex. Fcap. 8vo, cloth, ...	1	0
FIFTH STANDARD, 288 pp., Ex. Fcap. 8vo, cloth, ...	1	3
SIXTH STANDARD (for Boys), 352 pp., Ex. Fcap. 8vo, cl.,	1	6
SIXTH STANDARD (for Girls), 352 pp., Ex. Fcap. 8vo, cl.,	1	6
SIXTH STANDARD (for Mixed Classes), 480 pp., Ex. Fcap. 8vo, cloth, ...	2	0
HISTORY OF ENGLAND, for Junior Classes. By L. Schmitz, LL.D., London. Illustrated, Fcap. 8vo, cloth,	1	6
HISTORY OF SCOTLAND, for Junior Classes, with Map, and Illustrations, 192 pp., Fcap. 8vo, cloth, ...	1	0
HISTORY OF ENGLISH LITERATURE. By F. A. Laing. 256 pp., Extra Fcap. 8vo, cloth, ...	1	6
SPECIMENS OF ENGLISH LITERATURE — Prose. From the 14th to the 19th Centuries. Ex. Fcap. 8vo, cl.,	1	6
ELOCUTION IN THEORY AND PRACTICE. By J. A. Mair. 256 pp., Ex. Fcap. 8vo, cloth, ...	1	6
OUTLINES OF DOMESTIC ECONOMY FOR GIRLS. By J. Hassell, London. 150 pp., Extra Fcap. 8vo, cloth,	1	0
OUTLINES OF POLITICAL ECONOMY FOR SCHOOLS. By Dr. A. H. Dick. 160 pp., Extra Fcap. 8vo, cloth,	1	0
OUTLINES OF NATURAL PHILOSOPHY. By B. Simpson, London. 192 pp., Illustrated, Fcap. 8vo, cloth,	1	0
OUTLINES OF NATURAL HISTORY. By Dr. A. H. Dick. 192 pp., Illustrated, Extra Fcap. 8vo, cloth, ...	1	0
OUTLINES OF CHEMISTRY. By George Chaloner, London. 192 pp., Illustrated, Extra Fcap. 8vo, cloth,	1	0
YOUNG SCHOLAR'S SPELLING AND WORD BOOK. By Wm. Rice. 128 pp., Fcap. 8vo, cloth limp, 9d; cl,	1	0
TEXT-BOOK OF ENGLISH COMPOSITION, with Exercises. By Thomas Morrison, A.M. 160 pp., Post 8vo, cl.,	1	3
DICTIONARY OF DERIVATIONS OF THE ENGLISH LANGUAGE. 400 pp., 18mo, cloth, ...	1	0

London, Edinburgh, and Herriot Hill Works, Glasgow.

William Collins, Sons, & Co.'s Educational Works.

COLLINS' SCHOOL SERIES.

SCHOOL AND COLLEGE CLASSICS.

WITH INTRODUCTION AND NOTES, Fcap. 8vo,

		S.	D.
MILTON, - -	PARADISE LOST, Bks. I. & II. &c., sewed 9d; cl.	1	0
SHAKESPEARE,	TRAGEDY OF RICHARD II., sewed 9d; cl.,	1	0

Others in Preparation.

SCHOOL CLASSICS, with Introduction and Notes.

WORDSWORTH,	LYRICAL BALLADS, 32 pp., Fcap. 8vo, sewed,	0	2
COLERIDGE, -	ANCIENT MARINER, &c., 32 pp., Fcap. 8vo,	0	2
CAMPBELL, -	PLEASURES OF HOPE, 32 pp., Fcap. 8vo,	0	2

Others in Preparation.

LANGUAGES.

LATIN PRIMER, for Stands. IV., V., and VI., 32 pp., ea.	0	2
FRENCH PRIMER, for Stands. IV., V., and VI., 32 pp., ea.	0	2
GERMAN PRIMER, for Stands. IV., V., and VI., 40 pp., ea.	0	3

GEOGRAPHY.

MY FIRST GEOGRAPHY, 64 pp., 18mo, cloth, ...	0	4
ELEMENTS OF MODERN GEOGRAPHY, 4 Maps, 12mo, cl.	1	0
GEOGRAPHY, for Standards IV. and V. 2d. each, VI. ...	0	3
COUNTY GEOGRAPHIES OF ENGLAND AND WALES, ea.	0	2
COUNTY GEOGRAPHIES OF SCOTLAND, ... each	0	2
OUTLINES OF PHYSICAL GEOGRAPHY, 12mo, cloth,	1	0
PHYSICAL GEOGRAPHY, Stands. IV., V., VI., Maps, ea.	0	2

ARITHMETIC.

FIRST LESSONS IN ARITHMETIC, 36 pp., 18mo, ...	0	3
SYSTEM OF PRACTICAL ARITHMETIC, 18mo, cloth,	0	9
ARITHMETIC, Stands. I. II., ea. 1d.; III. IV., ea. 1½d.; V. VI. ea.	0	2
THE STANDARD ARITHMETIC, Ex. Fcap. 8vo, cloth,	1	0
COMPLETE SYSTEM OF ARITHMETIC, 192 pp., 12mo, cl.	1	6
ALGEBRA for Standards IV., V., and VI., 32 pp., each	0	2
ELEMENTS OF ALGEBRA, 48 pp., 12mo, cloth, ...	0	6
ELEMENTS AND PRACTICE OF ALGEBRA. By J. LOUDON, M.A. 277 pp., Fcap. 8vo, cloth, ...	2	6
EUCLID'S ELEMENTS, Books I. to VI., 12mo, cloth, ...	1	6
METRIC SYSTEM OF WEIGHTS AND MEASURES, with Solutions of the Questions for Examinations, 48 pp., cl.,	0	3
BOOKKEEPING, Single and Double Entry. By DR. BRYCE, Post 8vo, cloth, ...	1	6

London, Edinburgh, and Herriot Hill Works, Glasgow.

Collins' School Series.

OUTLINES

OF

POLITICAL ECONOMY.

BY

A. H. DICK, D.SC. (Edin.), M.A., LL.B. (Lond.)

LONDON AND GLASGOW:
WILLIAM COLLINS, SONS, & COMPANY.
1874.

PREFACE.

This little Volume aims at a clear statement of the leading principles of Political Economy; and such an explanation of them as the young may easily understand, and the old not unprofitably read. Few branches of human knowledge are so closely connected with the practical questions of daily life; and the work aims, therefore, not merely to lead to an understanding of these principles, but also to incite to the adoption of such a line of conduct in life, as shall be consistent with the truths taught.

Many and excellent as are the books which have been written on the subject, it is clear enough that there is room for more. One has but to think of the ignorance of the truths of the Science which is displayed in most conversations on Capital and Labour, and to take note of some of the proceedings of both parties in the struggle which is at present going on between these two, to see that—however well the truths of Political Economy may be known by a few—much has yet to be done before they permeate Society, so as to be the acknowledged basis for the rules and objects of our industrial combinations.

GLASGOW, *January, 1873.*

CONTENTS.

		PAGE
I.	SOCIETY,	7
II.	VALUE,	11
III.	MONEY,	14
IV.	WAGES,	20
V.	LABOUR,	25
VI.	DIVISION OF LABOUR,	30
VII.	CAPITAL,	35
VIII.	KINDS OF CAPITAL,	41
IX.	PROFITS,	45
X.	INTEREST,	50
XI.	MACHINERY,	55
XII.	THRIFT AND SPENDTHRIFT,	61
XIII.	PRICE,	65
XIV.	PROPERTY,	70
XV.	RENT,	75
XVI.	EDUCATION OF WORKMEN,	80
XVII.	COMPETITION,	85
XVIII.	TRADES UNIONS,	90
XIX.	CO-OPERATION,	98
XX.	TAXES,	103

		PAGE
XXI.	FREE TRADE,	108
XXII.	CREDIT AND BANKS,	113
XXIII.	PAPER MONEY AND SAVINGS BANKS,	118
XXIV.	INSURANCE AND POOR LAWS,	123
XXV.	INTEMPERANCE,	129
XXVI.	DIVISIONS OF POLITICAL ECONOMY,	135
XXVII.	THE OBJECT OF POLITICAL ECONOMY,	139
XXVIII.	PROTECTION: THE MAYOR OF ENIOS; AN ILLUSTRATION,	146
	EXERCISES ON THE LESSONS,	149
	DEFINITIONS AND EXPLANATIONS OF TERMS,	158

POLITICAL ECONOMY.

I.—SOCIETY.

WHY should men require to work? The lilies of the field and the birds of the air neither toil nor spin, and yet have enough for their wants. The flowers bloom, fruits ripen, and the young lions are provided for, without labour. Why, then, should our days be days of fatigue?

Too often is the workman tempted to ask such questions; and, unless he be willing to reflect and study carefully the workings of that society of which he forms a part, he finds it really difficult to answer them.

For one thing, the workman is a man—a being much higher in his nature than any plant or lower animal; he has feelings and desires that they can know nothing of, and a mind capable of pleasures such as they can never enjoy. Animals have few wants, and therefore require to take but little trouble to provide for them; plants, being unconscious things, have none. But man finds himself in a world which presents varied pleasures to his senses, and higher gratifications still to his intellect. To attain these he must bestir himself. He is so created that he must have food, clothing, home, health, safety, and diversion. Now, while the possession of these things is to him enjoyment, the want of them is painful. To avoid the pains and possess the pleasures he must make efforts. Work alone can supply his wants; work alone avert his dangers.

But another thing often perplexes the workman. Granting that work is needful, it seems to him as if he wrought not for himself, but for his employers. He sees them working but little with their hands, and yet abounding in good things, while he gets but a scanty pittance; and it is hard for him to understand why one gets so much for so little labour, and another so little for so much. In fact, society and its workings seem to him all wrong. He sees some who do nothing but sit still, while others, whose life is all toil, lay the products of that toil at their feet; and can hardly help thinking that society is a kind of arrangement of human beings by which the masses are compelled to serve the few who occupy high places.

But human society is not really so. It is an arrangement, the result of the experience of many centuries, by which men can live together, and every individual render service to every other according to his powers and circumstances. If the workman toils for his employer, others toil for him. If the master receives a large amount of wealth as the produce of all that his workmen do, the workman also receives a large amount of service in the living which his wage affords. The clothes which he wears, how came they there? Did not people in America cultivate cotton for his shirts? Were not these spun, and woven, and sewed by working people? Hindoos must have raised indigo to dye his jacket. South Americans must have hunted cattle to provide the leather for his shoes. Miners must have dug iron for the nails in them, as well as for the machinery by which the wool and cotton of his dress was spun and woven. Smelters must have smelted the iron, and engineers fitted up the machines. As he goes to his work he passes through streets which have been paved by workmen for his convenience; and, as he returns at night, they are lighted by others, that he may see. The bread he eats could not have been ready for him without the services of ploughman, reaper, miller, and baker. The tea he drinks is his through the united labours of Chinese cultivators, of merchants, shipowners, shipbuilders, ropemakers, canvas-weavers, sailors. The sugar with which he sweetens it has given employment to quite as many. Who could count all the people of whose services he and his family receive a share in any one day of their existence,—the pattern-designers, who drew the figure on his wife's dress and shawl; the straw-workers and milliners, who prepared her bonnet; the authors, printers, and publishers, who furnished his son with school-books; the joiners, who made the furniture of his house; the masons, plasterers, glaziers, and others, who built his house; the policeman, who watches it for him; the guard, stoker, driver, navvies, capitalists, who all work together to help him on his journey as he takes a trip by rail? And by what means does he command all these services, some of them done for him by people, it may be, long since dead? By his wages, which enable him to buy food, or books, or railway-tickets, or whatever else he can afford to buy. And what are his wages but money, which gives him the power of buying these services in return for the services he renders to his employer? By living and working among his fellow-men, he finds opportunity of rendering services to others, for which others are rendered back to him. This, then, we may say, is the great law which binds society—" Service for service."

For, it is plain that if a man lived alone, like Robinson Crusoe on his desert island, it would be utterly impossible to do for himself one-thousandth part of the things which he gets others to do for him in society. He would have to build his own hut, seek and cook his own food, carry water for himself, make his own furniture; and all of these things would be done in the most clumsy way, for few men can do more than one thing well. Many, too, of the commonest articles of every-day comfort, which are enjoyed in society, most men could not make at all. The same would be the case if men, though not on any desert island, had the habit of living apart from each other like the wild animals. It is only because they live together, one doing one thing, another another, and each readily exchanging with the rest some of the products of his work for a part of theirs,—it is only by such mutual interchange of services that society exists.

A blind man groping through the streets of a town, and suffering much because he had no guide, not even a dog, heard a lame man crying out in vain for some one to help him on his way. "My brother in misfortune," said he, "You suffer as well as I do. Let us help each other." "How can we do so," replied the lame man, "when I am unable to move a single step?" "True," said the blind man, "but then each of us has exactly what the other wants, I have sound legs and you have good eyes, I will carry you wherever you wish to go, and you will direct me where I should turn my steps." The friendly bargain was struck, and the wants of each were henceforth well supplied.

The union of mankind in society presents a similar kind of agreement,—not between two men, but between all the men of all the nations that have commercial dealings with each other. Each man, or each nation, serves others by producing things which they cannot produce as well for themselves, and receives services in return which neither the nation for itself, nor the man for himself, could so easily have done.

The conditions under which these products and services are exchanged between man and man, and between nation and nation, give rise to a great variety of relations between different classes of men, such as master and servant, landlord and tenant, lender and borrower, buyer and seller. The study of these relations, and of the laws which regulate the production, exchange, and division of goods among men, is the object of **Political Economy.**

Men labour to avoid pains and obtain comfort and pleasure.

The workman obtains a multitude of services from others as he spends his wages.

The law which binds society is "service for service." Men in society and nations are useful to each other by exchange of services.

II.—VALUE.

WHOEVER supplies any of my wants, or gives me the means of supplying them, renders me a service. The boatman who rows me over a ferry which I wish to cross, or the baker who gives me a loaf when I am hungry, both usually expect some service from me in return. It is true that the ferryman and the baker may, if they happen to be friends of mine, render me the service out of friendship; but no baker and no ferryman would, or could, do so to every man. They expect to be paid; and it is those services which men render to each other in the expectation that they will be repaid which we have to consider in the study of Political Economy—not such as a mother renders to her child, or friends to each other. These form a different and, it may be, a much higher study—that of morality; but we must leave them out of sight in studying the laws according to which men, who are total strangers, will work for each other. For, as we have seen, all of us use to a large extent the results of the work of persons whom we know nothing about. How can I tell who made the boots I am wearing, or who built the house I live in?

The ferryman expects to be repaid the value of his trouble; the baker the value of his loaf. How is the value of things or services to be estimated? It is clear that if I offer so little for the loaf that the baker would rather keep it; or if he asks so much that I would rather go without it, there can be no exchange or trading between us. The same thing is true in the case of the ferryman. Each of us in trading must have a benefit by the bargain. If the ferryman be too greedy, I can walk up the river bank to a point where it is shallow enough for me to cross without a boat and without need for payment; and he, on the other hand, will only row me across if I give him as much as will afford him a satisfaction sufficient for his labour in rowing the boat. There are thus two things which go to fix the value of the thing bought and sold, or of the service given and paid for: *first*, the amount of trouble saved to the person who receives the service or thing; *second*, the amount which the other will consider sufficient for making the thing, or for doing the service required.

Now, suppose that I had a wishing-belt like those mentioned in fairy tales, by means of which, whenever I wished myself in any place there I should be at once—is it likely that I should pay the ferryman to take me across the river? Or suppose that I had, like Aladdin, a lamp, by the mere rubbing of which I could immediately have a loaf or anything else I wish for—is it likely that I would higgle with the baker about his loaf? No! people will only pay for those things which they want, and which they cannot get without either buying or producing for themselves.

Here, then, we can easily see what kind of things or services have any value in the market, or in the dealings of one man with another. Not those which are to be had or found at any time; but those which are wanted, and yet not to be had without trouble. The man who does not want a loaf never dreams of paying for one; nor, if loaves were as plentiful as stones, would he pay for one; because, when he wanted it, he could pick it up from the road.

Some people think that it is because things are useful that men pay for them. But water, as we all know, is exceedingly useful, yet no one will pay anything for it where he can have it for drawing from a well close at hand. Air, too, is among the most useful things one can name; but we do not pay for it, because it is always at hand. Water and air are much wanted, we could not live without them; but because they are so plentiful they are not articles of exchange—of market-value. In the desert, however, where water is scarce, travellers, whose supply is exhausted, pay dearly to those who have some to dispose of; and in large towns, where it has to be brought from a distance, people pay for it. Those who are ill and can hardly breathe, pay willingly the fee of the physician who restores to them the power of inhaling the air freely. But it is not the usefulness of the water or of the air for which the payment is made; it is the services of those who have conveyed the water into the desert or into the town, and the service which the skill of the physician has rendered that is paid for.

Nor is it because things are beautiful that we give anything in exchange for them; though often one is apt to think so. Wild flowers are beautiful, but nature supplies us with them for nothing; while a painting of flowers, not half so lovely as the real flowers, is readily paid for, because it is not to be had without trouble. The usefulness or the beauty of certain things may, indeed, lead us to desire to possess them—to want them; but, in every case, that which has a value in the market, whether it be a service done or an article produced, has the value, not because it is useful—not because it is beautiful, but because people want it, and those who supply the want save them the trouble of supplying it themselves.

Therefore, what those who sell receive is payment for their services in producing the article sold; and what those who buy give is payment for being saved the trouble of producing it. That payment, if made in money, becomes to the seller a means of buying other people's services; and thus, again, we have the truth presented to us, that the bond of society is "Service for service." Thus, the **value** of any article or work is the amount of money or of service which can be had for it in the market. More strictly, this should be called the exchange value; for, not uncommonly, things are said to be valuable which people prize highly, though no one would give anything in exchange for them. A gift, or a keepsake, from a dead or distant friend, is often said to be of great value, although it would not fetch a shilling if sold; and, to a mother, the little shoe of her dead child may in one sense be said to be of infinite value, while, in truth, it has no exchange value at all, for no one would buy it. In all the following sections, when the word **value** is used, it must be understood to mean value in the market, or **exchange value.**

Since only those things which are wanted, and which it is difficult to obtain, have value, thus understood, it is easy to see what things will have most value—those, namely, which are most wanted; that is, for which the demand among men is greatest; and which at the same time require the greatest amount of trouble or service to procure; in other words, of which the supply is most limited.

The value of a service is what can be had in return for it. That which can be had without trouble has no value. That which is not wanted by any one has no value. Neither usefulness nor beauty are causes of value. The value of a service depends on the trouble saved to the receiver, and on the amount necessary to make the giver render it.

III.—MONEY.

IT is seldom that people exchange goods for goods, or services for goods, directly. When a man works for another, he expects **money** in return; and, when he gives goods to another, it is usually money which he expects and gets. This money represents all the goods with which he has parted, or the services which he has rendered to others, and those other goods or services which he may buy with it when he pleases. Money may thus be said to be the means by which men are enabled most conveniently to exchange goods and services—means without which such exchange could only be effected with great difficulty.

For, suppose there were no money in a country, then see what happens. A brewer, for example, has plenty of beer, but requires corn. In order to get this, he must carry his beer—no easy task—to a farmer who possesses corn. But the farmer, it may be, does not want beer; or, perhaps, he requires less value in beer than the brewer has need of in corn. The brewer must then seek out some other farmer who wants beer, and can give the corn he requires. It is clear that such a system of exchanging goods for goods can only be carried on under great difficulty. But worse cases than this must occur. Here, for example, is a cabinetmaker who has a sofa, and wants bread. How shall he get it? He does not want as much bread as shall be equal to his sofa in value; can he offer a bit of it to the baker? Here, again, is a sheep-farmer who possesses sheep, but wishes a pair of stockings, or a hat. How can he pay these by means of sheep? Kill one, it may be said, and give the hatter a part of it. But, perhaps, the farmer is not a butcher; and, since the mutton cannot be kept fresh, what is to become of the rest of it, unless the farmer happen to want exactly such a number of other goods as will be equal to the sheep's carcase in value, and can find, at once, people who will give him their goods for the different parts of it?

The exchange of goods for goods is called **barter**. Because of difficulties like those just mentioned, extensive commerce can never be carried on by means of barter; and it is the happy invention of money which has enabled people to exchange their goods and their services when they will, and in such quantities as they please. For the brewer can pay as much money to the farmer as will represent the value of the corn he requires; and the farmer can buy with part of the money, when he pleases, as much beer as he wants; and the cabinetmaker and the baker can each deal in the same way.

Let us consider, now, what kind of material is best fitted to serve as money. Some strange things have been used for it by different nations. The Chinese used cubes of pressed tea; some African tribes use shells; others use cattle, others salt; but modern civilized nations all use **gold** and **silver**, and most of them **copper**. What is it that makes them (especially gold and silver) so suitable for the purpose of exchange?

First, They are articles of great value. The trouble required to get them from the mines in mountainous countries, where alone they are found, is very great; and the demand for them is also great. If they were not valuable, people would not exchange other articles of value for them.

Secondly, They are of small bulk in proportion to their value. If it required large masses of them to be equal in value to the articles which they represent, then there would be nearly as much trouble in carrying them about, for the purpose of exchange, as we have seen in regard to a sheep or a sofa.

Thirdly, Gold and silver are easily divided into small fragments, and each fragment keeps its value in relation to the whole. The half of a piece of either of them will exchange for half of the goods which might be got for the whole; the fourth part, for the fourth part of the goods, and so on. Diamonds are of small bulk and of great value, but still they would not be useful as money; for, when one of them is broken into two, or into four parts, the halves or fourths are not exchangeable for nearly the half or fourth part of the goods which would be given for the whole diamond.

Fourthly, Gold and silver do not change their qualities readily. If they were apt to decay, like the farmer's mutton, then the money which a man had received in the morning would, at evening, exchange only for goods of less value than he had given for them.

Fifthly, Gold and silver do not, by a change in the supply of them, increase or diminish suddenly in value; for, as they are got with great labour from the bowels of the earth, they do not easily become more plentiful in the market, as corn does in a year of good crops, or more scarce, as the corn does in a bad year.

Sixthly, Since they are what the chemists call elements,—that is, unmixed substances,—they are always of the same quality and nature throughout their whole bulk;

so that the same quantity of either of these metals is always of the same value at the same time.

Seventhly, Gold and silver are malleable, and thus capable of receiving distinctly the impression or stamp which governments put upon pieces of them of different sizes, in order to make coins of them, and to mark their purity, so that people may receive them with confidence in exchange for goods or services.

Eighthly, They are hard, and the government stamp endures upon them for a long time.

Copper is useful as money for similar reasons; and as it is of less value, that is, more easily got, than gold and silver, it serves better for representing small quantities of other things, and thus aids in the exchange of such small quantities as, without it, would require the aid of very small pieces of gold or silver.

Since the value of a thing is what can be got in exchange for it, the value of money is the quantity of any other kind of goods which can be had in exchange for a given amount in gold or silver coins. When we compare other things with these, we call the amount of the coins given for them the **price**. Thus, we may say, a shilling is the price of a pound of butter. Suppose now that two pounds of sugar are exchanged for a shilling, then it is clear that one pound of butter is equal in value to two pounds of sugar. Money therefore serves as a standard for measuring the values of all kinds of goods and services. Now, the sum of all the goods and services which a nation or an individual can command is called the **wealth** of that nation or individual; and thus we see that money is, on the one hand, a **representative**, and, on the other, a **measure of wealth**.

But money must not, in itself, be regarded as wealth. Wealth consists only of such kinds of goods and such kinds of services as can supply human wants; and in this sense, as much of the gold and silver in the world as exists in the shape of chains, watches, plate, and ornaments may be said to be wealth; but in the form of money gold and silver are essentially the representative and the measure of wealth. The measure of anything is not the thing itself. What measures cloth is not cloth; a clock is not time. Bread, meat, coals, sugar, these are wealth: these supply our wants. But no man is fed by money, warmed or clothed with gold coins, nursed in his sickness by silver ones. As we shall see in a future section, the law makers of old times made serious mistakes through confounding money with wealth; and brought famines and rebellions into our country by passing laws which hindered gold from being taken out of it; and corn, and cloth, and other things, which would have supplied the necessities of the people, from being brought into it. The legislators of Great Britain are wiser now; and our laws have of late been framed under the just belief that it matters little whether there be more or less money in the country, if the cupboards of the people contain bread enough, the larders meat enough, the presses cloth enough, and the cellars coal enough.

We must keep clearly in our minds the difference between the price and the value of a thing. We shall do this all the better, if we remember that there may be a general rise or fall in the prices of goods; but there cannot be a general rise or fall in their values. For the price of anything is the amount of gold or silver for which it can be exchanged; and its value is the amount of every other thing taken singly which it can be exchanged for. If half of all the gold and silver in the country were destroyed, other things remaining the same in quantity, all these other things would be exchanged in given quantities for only half of the gold and silver for which they were exchanged before; and thus there would be a general fall in the prices of them. If all the gold and silver in the country were doubled in amount, other things remaining the same, then all these other things would be exchanged in given quantities, for double the amount of the gold and silver for which they were previously exchanged; and thus there would be a general rise of prices.

But if half the existing quantity of everything exchangeable in the country, including gold and silver, were suddenly destroyed, then everything left would be exchanged in exactly the same quantity of one thing for the same quantity of another as before; and thus there would be no change of values. People would, in regard to all things, be only half as wealthy as before. The same thing, as regards values, would be true, if the quantity of everything exchangeable were suddenly doubled; only people would be twice as wealthy as before.

Although gold, silver, and copper are all used as money in Great Britain, gold forms what is called the standard coin of the country. People cannot, without confusion, have two different standards by which to measure anything, whether it be cloth, land, or wealth. It is not lawful to offer payment of large sums in anything but gold. For, if it were lawful to pay them in either gold or silver, then those who had large amounts to pay would pay them in silver when silver happened to be low in value, or in gold when it happened to be low. Some people think it would be an advantage to make it lawful to pay large amounts either in gold or silver as one pleased—that is, to have a **double standard** of value; but only the **single standard,** gold, is allowed. In Great Britain no man may pay more than forty shillings in silver, or more than five shillings in copper.

A man's wealth is the amount of goods and services to which he has a right. Money is not wealth; it only represents and measures wealth. It saves commerce from the difficulties of barter.

Gold and silver are adapted for coins because they are of great value in small bulk; easily divided; not liable to change; the same throughout their whole mass; malleable, and hard.

There may be a general rise or fall of prices; but there cannot be a general rise or fall of values.

The single standard of gold, and not the double standard of gold and silver, is lawful in Great Britain.

IV.—WAGES.

When men do any kind of work they generally merely move matter from one place to another, so that materials which before were unconnected are joined together, and others which before were joined are separated. A baker brings particles of flour, water, butter, sugar, yeast, eggs, and other things together; removes them from the baking table to the oven; takes them out from the oven after a time, and then his cake is made. A tailor tears large pieces of cloth into small pieces; then puts these together in a certain way, and makes a needle pass through them at certain places, leaving a thread where it has passed; and so his coat is made. A night-watchman, by moving up and down on his beat, scares away rogues from honest men's houses. A teacher moves the air with his organs of voice; and so does a singer at a concert. A corn merchant brings corn in ships from one country to another. A retail shopkeeper carries goods in large quantities from the wholesale merchant's store to his own shop, and there divides them into small parcels suitable for poor people and daily use. And so it might be shown that all work is only some mode of moving pieces of matter; whatever else is needed to make matter into goods fit for the use of men is done by what we call the forces of nature. Nay, it is with good reason that men think that all the wondrous works of nature—the changes which we call mechanical, or chemical, or electric—are themselves only modes of movement of exceedingly small particles of matter.

In doing these things we see that men render services to each other. The services of the baker are shut up, as it were, in the loaf; those of the tailor in the coat. Those whose services are thus embodied in some useful object, which can be seen and handed from one to another, are usually called **productive** labourers. But in what are the services of the night-watchman, the teacher, and the singer embodied? There is no material object in which they can be seen. Again, in what are the services of the corn importer, of the carrier, and of the retail shopkeeper embodied? Not in the corn or in the contents of the parcel. These are the same in the country or town to which they are brought, as they were in that from which they were brought; and the same when divided into small, as when in large quantities. All of these men, whose services are not embodied in any useful material object, are called usually **unproductive labourers**—a most improper name, since it is clear they must have produced something of value, or men would not pay them for their labours. Their services, beyond a doubt, produce satisfaction of one kind or another—supply some want which men feel. The night-watchman gives us safety; the teacher, knowledge; the singer, pleasure; and a hungry man in Britain about to eat a cake can easily tell you the want which the man has supplied who brought the flour from Odessa in bags or barrels. To those who think that all labourers are productive or unproductive, the man who makes a fiddle is a productive labourer, while the man who plays upon it, no matter how sweetly, is an unproductive labourer. Those who, like the corn importer and the shopkeeper, convey goods that embody the services of others to the people who use or consume them, are sometimes called **intermediaries**. Their services come in between the production and the consumption of the goods; but still it should be remembered that they are not the less services for which men pay.

We are apt to think, when we buy and pay for a loaf, that it is the baker only whom we are paying, and that the value is something contained in the loaf itself; and so, when we buy a coat, we think we pay the tailor only, and that the value lies in the coat. But it is all the men who helped to make the loaf or the coat that we pay, and not merely the tailor or the baker; and it is the services which are embodied in the loaf or the coat for which we pay, and not the loaf or the coat itself. In the loaf are shut up the services not only of the baker, but also of the miller, the sower, the reaper, the ploughman, and many others. In the coat are shut up the services not only of the tailor, but also of the weaver, spinner, wool-carder, sheep-farmer, and more than one can well name. And it is these we pay for, not the material object itself, except because it contains these, and could not be got by us without them.

There is hardly anything in political economy which it is more important that we keep in memory than this: that it is not things we pay for, but the services rendered to us in giving us these things,—the trouble men have taken in producing them, and have saved to us who are the purchasers. We pay for neither the matter of the loaf, nor of the plant from which the flour that made the loaf came, nor for the living power of the plant, nor for the powers of the soil, or the air, or the sunshine which made the plant grow; we pay only the services of those who took pains to enclose and cultivate the soil, and reared the plants in places where air and water and sunshine could get at them and nourish them. The powers of the soil and the air and the water are gifts of nature,—given for nothing to those who first enclosed the ground, and which are given for nothing still, to all who will search for and enclose new lands, or who will expose plants where the air and sunshine can get at them. Such services have no value in the market, as is easily seen in regard to the air, the water, and the sunshine. It is only men's services which have a value; and the object of political economy, as a science, is to increase the number of free services which nature can render us, and make needless those of men, which cost so much,—to make nature work for us rather than men in increasing our wealth.

The price paid for all the services of all the men engaged in producing anything of value is called its **cost of production;** and the act of rendering these services is called **labour.** Labour, then, and the forces of nature, are the sources of all our wealth; from one or other of these, or from both united, come all the goods and services which any nation or individual can command. You will often hear it said that labour and land are the sources of wealth; but those who so speak of land mean by it all the powers of nature which the land is a means of bringing to act upon plants, or of hiding in minerals. To speak correctly, nature and labour are the sources of wealth; and the work of nature in the production of wealth is free, that of labour must be paid.

Every time that two articles of value are exchanged, men are really purchasing from each other services rendered by labour, and shut up in the things exchanged. Whether we buy goods, or pay performers, or pay carriage of goods, or a railway fare, it is really labour that we purchase. The buying of a loaf differs in nothing of importance from the engagement of a man to do work; and the man who asks for employment is doing the same thing in reality as the man who wants to sell his goods. The one seeks to sell labour directly, the other to sell it as contained in his goods.

Now, what is paid for labour of any kind is called **wages**. We are apt to speak of the payment given to the common day labourer only as wages; and we give finer names to the payments which are made for some other kinds of services. Thus we speak of the doctor's or the lawyer's fee; of the judge's salary; of the teacher's income; of the merchant's profit; of the banker's interest; and of the professor's emoluments. They are all, in reality, only payments for labour of different kinds, or for different results of labour,—that is, they are all wages.

Why are the wages of some men so very great, while others are so poorly paid? and why are the wages of the same man high at one time and lower at another? These questions can easily be answered by those who know why wild flowers can be got for nothing, and artificial flowers cost money. Whatever kinds of labour are easily got, because the labourers are numerous, for these little will be paid. Whatever kinds of labour are scarce, because those who can do such labour are not easily found, for these high wages will be paid. Let us consider then what circumstances make tradesmen of some kinds numerous, and of others scarce.

First, Few people like to work at a trade that is disagreeable,—such as that of a chimney-sweeper, or a collier, or a needle-maker. The first is dirty, the second dirty and dangerous, and the third unhealthy. For this reason the number of such workmen is small, compared with the number of the people who require their services. The supply of such kinds of labour is small, and the demand for them great, for almost everybody requires needles, coals, and chimneys swept; therefore these trades are highly paid.

Second, Few people have the means of learning trades which require great skill, because few have the means of paying teachers of such kinds of work. The larger number of workmen are therefore obliged to go to some easily learnt trade. On this account there are few surgeons, or architects, or lawyers; but many ploughmen, weavers, coachdrivers, policemen, and the like. The services of the first are difficult to obtain, and therefore highly paid; the others are poorly paid, because, though their services are wanted, they are easily got.

Third, Few people like to enter trades in which employment is not constant,—such as those of a mason or a bricklayer, who is stopped by every frost. Therefore such trades are well paid.

Fourth, There are unfortunately but few men in whom great trust can be reposed; the services therefore of such are highly paid,—as those, for example, of bankers, of confidential clerks, or of jewellers' assistants.

Fifth, Few men care to engage in a profession in which success is uncertain and rare. For this reason successful artists, actors, and book-writers earn enormous sums; but the route to success in such professions is strewn with the wrecks of those who have tried them and miserably failed.

Labour and the forces of nature produce all wealth. All labour is but the movement of particles of matter from one place to another.

Men pay for services, not strictly for the goods in which services are contained. The price of all the services contained in goods is called their cost of production. Wages are payment for labour of any kind.

Wages are high in trades that are disagreeable or dangerous, difficult to learn, inconstant as employments, require trustworthiness, and uncertain as to success; because labourers in such trades are difficult to obtain.

V.—LABOUR.

LABOUR and the forces of nature are the sources of wealth; and since nature only gives her powers where labour is bestowed to secure them, it is clearly one of her laws, that by labour only shall men live. They who do not work shall not eat. There is no escape from this unless one will steal and eat what another has worked for. There are men who call themselves reformers and philanthropists, whose proposals of change seem to promise greater wealth for the labouring classes by means of some wonderful new arrangement of society—some mixture of the force of law and the sweetness of brotherly love, which it is very difficult to understand. The plain English of what they say is, that what one man has must be taken from him and given to another. Now, he who promises to any class of men higher wages, without requiring that they shall do more work, or work more skilfully, is either a fool or an impostor. In the same way, he who proposes to make all men's wages equal, for that too is wished by some, and does not at the same time show how all men's work can be made equal in quantity and skill—proposes to rob the active and skilful workmen, in order to give his plunder to the slothful and dull.

It is labour that creates the wealth of the world, but not mere hand labour. Your manual labourer often speaks as if his class alone produced the riches, which, it is too true, his class seldom enjoys. He speaks of those who work only with pens or drawing tools, who think and invent, as the drones of society, that live and prey upon its hard working hand labourers. Those who speak so forget that the high pay of the man who labours with his mind is got only because his services are more valuable to the world than those of the hand-worker—they are more in demand and more difficult to be got. And no wonder that the world so judges of them. For see, by invention and thought, one can now grind as much corn as a hundred and fifty could, in those ancient times when hand-workers sat and ground it between two stones. By the invention and thought of the barber Arkwright, one man can now do more in cotton-spinning than many hundreds could do before he thought out and invented his machines. It is true that hand-workers spend their strength in the creation of wealth, and have a right to their share; but what that share ought to be, because of their strength, may be judged of by him who remembers that the steam-engines now at work in Great Britain exert more strength than one-third of all the strength of all mankind. Shall not men rate the services of those whose thoughts and inventions put such force at their disposal higher than those of mere hand-workers? It is the intelligence which a man can put into his labours that alone can render his services valuable in those days of iron and steam; and even that must be of a high kind if he wishes to be highly paid. For if a man works at a trade which requires no great amount of intelligence or skill, he will find that iron and steam can do that as well as he can, and better even, as well as cheaper. Machines can count numbers; machines can tell the quantity of liquor drawn from a cask; machines can measure cloth or ribbons; machines can tell how many people enter an omnibus or an exhibition; such kinds of labour can never be highly paid, for the services they render can be got wherever .iron and water can be had.

Nor do those who work with their brain rather than their hands get their high wages by any kind of unjust law or government authority. It must be remembered that the price given for anything is only what the purchasers are willing to give for it, to save themselves trouble, not what the seller demands. The opinion of the purchaser is the real test of value, and since no man is forced to buy in a free country, there is no injustice done where those whose services are easily got or easily done for one's self receive small pay; and those whose services are much wanted and hard to obtain are highly paid. The great lesson that all of us may learn from this is to devote our time to study and to qualify ourselves as far as we can to render services to the world of a kind which neither ignorance nor machinery can do. In Great Britain workmen are not slaves like those of ancient Rome, and Greece, and Egypt; nor serfs like those of European countries some centuries ago; but free to choose their own occupation, and free to reap the highest rewards which they can induce society to give them for the work they do themselves, or for the services they can render to it, when they constrain the chemical, mechanical, and electric powers of nature to aid them in their work.

Wages depend upon the **supply** and **demand** in regard to labour. Now those who supply labour are in fact the population, since almost the whole of a people must work in one way or other. If a country have too large a population, their wages must be low as a whole, however they may differ in different trades; for the people will strive against each other to obtain employment and the means of living. According to a writer, named Malthus, all civilized countries are likely sooner or later to have more human beings in them than can live comfortably, and even the whole world may one day be too crowded. For human beings, Malthus tells us, are apt to increase in numbers faster than the means of feeding them will grow. Unless care is taken by mankind to prevent such an overcrowding, nature does it, and reduces the numbers by the cruel means of famine and pestilence; and the evil passions of men help nature by means of wars. These are what are called the positive checks upon overcrowding. Of course, men may do something by inventing plans to make the earth yield more fruit, the sea more fish, and the air more fowl. And when we think of the vast plains on the globe yet untouched by the spade or the plough,—of the valleys of the Amazon, the Niger, and the Mississippi, we can almost afford to smile at the fears of Mr. Malthus.

But though the day of overcrowding for the whole world may be far enough off, too many people may huddle themselves up into a corner of the globe, and prefer to remain fixed in one country like plants, rather than seek another with fewer mouths and more food. It is certainly the interest of the working men of Britain that there should not be in the land too many of them, for their wages must be low. How shall the numbers of the people be kept down?

The advice of Malthus is that people should not enter into early and foolish marriages. The number of families would then be less, and fewer children would grow up to reduce wages by increasing the quantity of labour. This is certainly good advice. What can be more foolish than some of the marriages one sees of men and women who have saved no money with which to bring up their children; who, indeed, can do little more than provide the feast and hire the cabs for their marriage festival? and what can be more pitiful than to see the children of poor, and perhaps prodigal, parents in rags and dirt and want? In Norway, it is said, the peasants do not marry till they own a farm and money enough to stock it; and the Norwegian peasants are all well off.

Again, a country may avoid being overcrowded if the people accustom themselves to live well, and think the means of living well as important as living at all. Those who are content with one kind of the cheapest food, as the Irish were with potatoes, marry too early, for housekeeping is then easily begun. Their children grow up to be men and women, make labourers plentiful, and wages low; and then, when the food they are content with fails, as potatoes did in the year 1846, such a people's sufferings are terrible. They have no other still cheaper food upon which they can fall back. Potatoes failed at the same time in England; but the English people did not suffer so much, for they were used to wheaten bread. The Hindoos are liable to similar sufferings with the Irish; they live chiefly upon rice.

Another means of limiting the number of the working classes is that of **emigration**; and certainly the man is a fool who stays in his own country to feed on potatoes and fish, while he might, with equal or less labour, find wheaten bread, bacon, and tea in another. The difficulty in the way of emigration is that it requires that the emigrant should possess the means of paying a passage to America or Australia for himself and his family; and how is he to find them, if his wages have only been sufficient for bare life? Those who cannot save, cannot emigrate; and those who can and will save, are citizens such as a country should try to keep at home, not force to go abroad.

But there is, on the whole, no great danger of overpopulation for Great Britain, now that food can come to it free of taxes from every other country of the world. There is more danger of particular trades being overcrowded with workmen, by sudden changes of fashion, which cause the goods made by hundreds of workmen to be no longer in demand. This has been the case lately in the trade of those who made crinoline wires, and also in that of straw-plaiting. The same thing happens when a machine is invented which does the work of many men. The goods remain in demand, indeed; but the men and their work do not. This has happened in many trades, and it was long before the evil found its remedy. There is, indeed, hardly any remedy but one,—namely, that the workmen should so be educated as to be able, with greater ease, to turn from a trade that has failed them to something new.

The advice of Malthus is not applicable to all lands. There are countries which have too few inhabitants, and where an increase of population is an advantage. This is the case with most newly settled Colonies. Food and comfort is scarce in them, not because the land is not rich enough, but because there are so few people, that one man has to do many kinds of work, and does them all roughly and imperfectly. Labour cannot be properly divided. We shall see the effects of this in our next lesson.

Manual labour is of less value than labour of the mind, because intelligence is scarcer than strength. Machines can exert more strength than human beings, and can do work requiring limited intelligence quite as well.

Wages depend upon population. Malthus taught that the world is in danger of being overcrowded. Emigration, avoidance of early marriage, and living well, are hindrances to overcrowding of a country.

New Colonies suffer from want of population.

VI.—DIVISION OF LABOUR.

SINCE the wages of the labourer, whether he be of high or low degree,—a judge on the bench or a riveter in a boatyard,—depend upon his efficiency in producing such goods and services as men will pay him for, it is clearly each man's interest to seek out for himself that kind of labour in which he can produce most, and for which he is best fitted in mind and body. One man can do well what another cannot; and it needs no long study to perceive that, if every man were set to do whatever he is best fitted for, the world would have the best possible supply of goods and services. This is what is meant by division of labour. We have seen already how many workers of different kinds must have joined their efforts before we could have the common things used in any one day of our existence. The daily comforts of all civilized nations are mainly the result of division of labour. Savages have but little of it among them. Half-civilized nations, like Egypt of old and India, had it to a certain extent, and formed themselves into castes of different kinds of workers; but did not allow each workman to choose the kind of labour for which he was best fitted. The son was obliged to follow the trade of his father. It is the division of labour, together with the freedom that each man has to select his own special part of the division, which has given to Britain and other modern nations their wondrous commerce, as well as their perfection in producing articles of value. In fact, division of labour can only be carried on to a great extent where men have learnt to trust each other, and to work together for a common object, while they each choose their own separate parts of the work. For it is only for the sake of better uniting all their separate labours into one article of value that they divide at all. The shepherd rears and feeds sheep; the cutler makes shears to clip the wool; the spinner spins it; the weaver weaves it; the dyer dyes it; the tailor sews it; the shopkeeper retails it;—each does but the one thing, and all conspire to make a coat ready for the back of the consumer.

This book we are now reading contains the separate labours of very many workers united. A writer wrote the copy; a reader revised it, and divided it among compositors; they set the types; some one corrected the proofs; pressmen printed the sheets off; one adjusted the press; a boy fitted in the sheets; others squeezed and smoothed them after they were printed; girls folded them; others stitched them; a man cut the edges; another fixed the boards; another stretched and fixed the cloth; and another put the name upon the back. And these were not all; for there were ink-makers, paper-makers, and many more, tedious to mention.

In wise division and wise union of labour lies the secret of making things good and cheap. For, see what gain there is in wise division of labour:—

First, By doing only one thing, the workman acquires quickness of hand and eye. He gets what we call the knack of doing it well.

Second, By doing only one thing, he wastes no time in finding and adjusting the different tools which would be required to do a number of different things.

Third, When any article can be made by the combination of a great number of distinct processes, each of which is in itself simple, then these processes may be easily done by machinery. Thus division of labour leads to the invention of machines.

Fourth, When work is divided, each workman can be paid the right value of his work. Those who do the easy parts, which require no thought, can be paid according to their deserts; while those whose work requires skill and learning, can be paid higher. If the same man were to do all, his whole time would require to be paid at the rate which his skill would secure for him, and the time he spent in doing easy work would be wasted.

Fifth, The division of labour into processes that are easy, and processes that are difficult, enables all to find employment. If each workman did all the processes, then none could be employed but those who were able for them all,—for lifting heavy weights as well as for minute ingenious toil. For the young and weak there would be no work.

All kinds of workers find division of labour to their advantage. In old times, when men first studied science, the same man studied all the sciences together. He was an astronomer, a mental philosopher, a naturalist, a mathematician, a moral philosopher, and many other things all in one. Now, men choose a single branch of study and devote themselves to it, and both the sciences and the men are the better for it. Teachers were once, and are yet, teachers of everything,—reading, writing, arithmetic, grammar, geography, history, and classics.

Those teachers do best, however, who have each his own special subject; and those countries are best taught where the work of teaching is so divided.

Wise union of labour is as important as wise division. Many men must first work separately to build a ship, they must work together to launch and navigate it. Two men can lift a weight which one could hardly move. Two policemen may catch a thief, where one could not help his escaping. Ten fields joined into one farm may, because they are joined, be nearly as easily cultivated as one. The farmer of the whole ten would employ machinery, which the farmer of only one could not afford to do; for machines are costly, and can only be employed where a large quantity of labour is required.

It is a question easier asked than answered, whether large or small farms be best; but it is a question regarding the division and union of labour. The answer depends upon what one means by best. If by best you mean most productive, then in countries not yet wholly cultivated, like the United States, large farms are best. For machinery, as we have said, can be employed upon them. A large farmer can always spare ground and men to try new experiments in agriculture, a small farmer cannot. Division of labour can be extensively applied among the hands employed on a large farm, and much can be saved in fences and buildings.

If, by best, you mean best for the men employed, morally, and as citizens, then small farms, where the farmer is the owner are best. For these **peasant proprietors**, as they are called, will work hard on their own lands, will resist all violent changes in the state, will be manly, brave, honestly proud, and patriotic. But, let us notice, that to double the labour on a farm does not give nearly the double of the produce; so that the hard *intensive* labour of the peasant proprietor yields less for the common good and the cheapening of farm produce, than the *extensive* culture of a large farmer. On the other hand, where the products of a country are such as require close and careful watching, like the vines and olives and beet-root of France, small farms yield most produce.

Small farms are bad where the farmers are not the owners, but only labourers and yearly tenants, at excessive rents, and without security that they will be allowed to remain long enough to reap the advantage of any improvements they make. This was the kind of tenancy called **cottier tenure,** common in Ireland till recently. Under such a system improvements were never made, tenants were slothful, and land unproductive. In short, in some cases small farms are good, in others large ones; in some the one are bad, in some the other. In fact, the manner in which farms are held by tenants, that is, the kind of tenure has as much to do with the productiveness of farms as their size has. If a farmer have his farm on a **lease,** that is, on a tenure for a number of years, he is more likely to make improvements on it than he would be if he holds it only for one year, or on a short lease. And if he have a right to payment for improvements, such as drains and new buildings, he is exceedingly likely to do all that he thinks will make the land productive. The tenure in Irish farms, called **Ulster tenant right,** is one by which a farmer, on leaving a farm, receives from the next tenant a valuation for the abiding improvements which he has made. By what is called the **allotment system** small plots of ground are made highly productive. These are plots cultivated as gardens by labourers on their own account after their regular work is done. They serve as a pastime for town workmen; but some say they tend to lower the wages which the men can earn at their regular trades, by making it possible for them to live on a smaller wage, as they can live partly on the produce of the allotment.

Division of labour applies to countries as well as to tradesmen or farmers. The whole of the **commerce** of the world hinges upon the fact that different countries produce different useful and exchangeable products. Great Britain yields iron and coal at little cost; Poland and Russia yield corn without much labour; France and Spain yield wines and fruits. Each has its own natural product on easy terms, and could not produce what the others have without excessive labour, perhaps not at all. Clearly, then, the one wise thing for the inhabitants of each of these countries to do is to give themselves to the business for which nature has adapted their lands; the British to working with coal and iron, the Russians to raising corn, the French and Spaniards to the cultivation of the vine; and then each and all of them to the exchange of their respective goods. Simple and advantageous as it seems, that countries should thus divide their labours in production, and unite them in commerce, people were long in finding it out, and the Governments of some countries cannot, or will not, understand it yet.

By wise division and wise union of labour goods are produced cheaply. Division of labour gives the workman quickness of hand and eye, saves time, leads to invention of machinery, to fairness of payment, and to employment for all degrees of strength and ability.

Small farms are good when the tenants are owners, or have long leases; large farms are good when the land is fertile; they admit of division of labour and employment of machinery. The productiveness of farms depends partly upon their tenure.

Division of labour applies to nations, because different countries yield different products.

VII.—CAPITAL.

LABOUR, and a wise division of labour, are necessary that work be done efficiently. There is yet another thing necessary, and that is capital. Here, let us suppose, are a house to be built, and a number of workmen who have agreed to divide the labour among them. A year must elapse before the house can be finished, and the price claimed from the owner. Some of these workmen have plenty of tools, and provisions upon which they can live well enough till the end of the year; these tools and provisions have been saved from their former earnings, or given to them by others who had saved them. Others of the workmen have nothing but their hands and their skill. What arrangement will be made under such circumstances? The unprovided workmen will say to the others, "We are willing to give our services in the building of this house, but we cannot wait a whole year without receiving our reward. We must live in the meantime, and so must our wives and children. Besides, there is a risk that the person for whom the house is to be built may be unable to pay, and another purchaser may not be found at once. We desire to risk no such loss, and would prefer to have the means of life secure now. We will give up our right to an equal share of the price, if you, the more fortunate workmen, will provide us with tools, and give us as we go on a fixed payment, weekly or daily. You will have your chance of a larger sum when the house is paid for; we, in the meantime, shall have lived by our work."

The arrangement thus proposed is exactly the one which is adopted in society, without any formal proposal between employers and labourers. The employers are the workmen who have saved tools and provisions, or money to buy them. They wait for their reward till the goods are finished and paid for, and receive at the end naturally a larger sum than the common labourers; for they are paid for the use of the tools or of the money which bought them, and for the use of the money which bought the provisions, in addition to the wages of their labour. The money they have thus laid out in advance is called **capital**.

There are, then, two kinds of producers,—**capitalists** and **wage-receivers**, or **labourers**. It is clear that the one is as needful as the other,—capital as labour. To till a field, it is as needful to have the plough and some one who will give the ploughman food till harvest comes, as it is to have the ploughman himself. That some one is a capitalist in reality, whether you call him farmer, or landowner, or any other name. And whatever be the kind of goods produced by their united efforts,—whether grain, or houses, or cloth,—the price of them when finished must be such as will pay both labourer and capitalist.

Men must labour to receive wages; but they must save some of what they have earned by their labour, or they can have no capital. Capital is the result of savings. Where there is no disposition to save, there is misery. The people of the Polar regions get seals and fish in abundance during their long summer daylight. Then they live truly upon the fat of the land; but they lay past nothing for their six months of cold and darkness. The winter comes, and with it famine and death to the poor thriftless wretches. The slopes of the Andes, in Chili, produce vines with very little trouble. During the vintage the people are mostly drunk; and it is unpleasant, if not dangerous, to travel among them. The result is, that, except at the vintage season, the people have nothing but water to drink. The nakedness of the savages of Africa or Australia is not a state that they choose, but one they have not the sense to prevent by working steadily, and saving the means of purchasing clothes. That they would be glad to have them they show when they can get hold of an old coat, or a battered hat, by wearing them, often with nothing else. From the want of will to save among savage nations, they are gradually dying off before the presence of thriftier colonists. Men who can work and save, and have ships and guns, are edging them out of the world.

But, though capital is savings, all savings are not capital. Only such savings as are used for future production are so. The food that I lay past to-day, in order to eat to-morrow, as I lie in the sunshine, is something saved certainly; but it is not capital. Suppose that an Indian lives with a wife and children under a shady rock, amid tropical fruit trees, which yield him and them plenty of vegetable food; and that, about a day's journey off, there is a hunting-ground, in which he can at times catch and kill an animal, whose flesh serves to vary their vegetable diet. The fruit and the flesh may be said to form his wealth, at least after the one has been plucked and the other hunted, even though he intend to consume them the same day. Suppose, however, that part of the fruit and flesh be laid aside for next day's use, as he and his family rest, then that part will be savings, but not capital. But, suppose again, that he begins to think the way to the hunting-ground long, and the carrying home a dead animal tiresome; and that, looking at the river which flows past his hut, he says to himself, "I shall lay aside a week's fruit and flesh, and shall make a canoe during the week, to help me easily to the hunting-ground, and in bringing back whatever I kill,"—the reserve which he lays aside to support him while making the canoe is capital.

In London and Berlin and Paris there are large museums filled with the works of famous sculptors and painters; there are magnificent churches and extensive libraries; there are concert halls with instruments of the richest tone; costly monuments to great men, and splendid palaces. These form part of the wealth of their respective nations, they are the results of the savings of former generations of English, French, and Germans; but they are not capital. They are not used to produce other objects of value.

In Birmingham, Glasgow, Manchester, New York, and Lyons, there are factories, and steam-engines, shops, stores, warehouses, and railway stations, and between these and other cities are long lines of railway, and telegraph wires; all those have cost enormous sums of money. They, too, form part of the wealth of the country in which they are; they, too, are the result of savings, and they are capital. They are all used to produce other goods or services, not kept for their own sakes.

A farmer's capital is his drains, manures, seeds, ploughs, and harrows, and everything which he uses to bring forth the fruits of the earth; a manufacturer's is his steam-engines, cotton, wool, or other raw materials; a merchant's, his warehouses, shops, ships, and all the goods contained in them; and to all these we must add the money in their possession which is meant to be paid as wages.

It is sometimes said that wages depend upon two things, namely, **population** and **capital**. For this to be strictly true, capital would mean only such savings as were to be used in payment of wages. But all the things we have just named are capital also, and they do not in any way help to increase wages, for they are not paid to workmen. Again, and more correctly, it is said, "wages depend upon population, and that portion of the capital of a country which is destined to be paid for labour." The money which is supposed to be so destined is called the **wages fund**, and may be considered, according as it is a large or a small sum, to show the amount of the desire of those who possess it to employ workmen. In reality, then, the statement that wages depend upon population and the wages fund is only another way of saying what we have learned before, that the wages of labourers are higher, the more there are who desire their work and the fewer there are of themselves; and low, the more there are of themselves and the fewer of their would-be employers. The same thing is commonly and shortly expressed by saying that "wages depend upon the demand for, and the supply of, labour."

It should not be thought, however, that there is any such thing as a fixed sum of money in the country, forming a wages fund. There are times when people save more than at others, and men will withdraw money from trade more readily at one time than another, so that the sum of money in the country which goes to pay for labour must be always changing.

The capital which is paid as wages goes, in general, to buy food and clothing for the labourer. It ceases to exist longer as capital, having been consumed by the labourer. There is therefore a connection between wages and the price of food and clothing; and some people say that when prices are low, wages fall; when they are high, wages rise. Wages however depend entirely, as we have said, upon the supply of, and demand for, labour; and yet it may often be found true that a fall in the prices of food and clothing is followed by a fall of wages. The reason of this is the want of prudence of the labouring people. Whenever food and clothing become cheap they need to spend less upon them, and have plenty of money. They get married in such times without due reflection, and their children grow up to increase the number of labourers. It may also be true that at times high prices cause a rise of wages. The dearness of food and clothing leads to want on the part of the poor; want leads to sickness and death. If many labourers die, the supply of labour will be less; and, then, if there be no change in the demand, wages must rise.

People sometimes speak of a glut of capital. If they mean anything at all by the words, it is that there is too much capital in the country. But surely there can never be, in any country, too much food and clothing for its working men, too many tools and instruments to help them in doing their work. The more capital there is, the better for everybody; the better, beyond a doubt, for those who have saved it; and the better, too, for the labourers, since it makes the demand for labour all the greater.

Capital is savings which are applied to future production. The wages fund is the part of capital meant to be employed in the payment of labour. It is not a fixed quantity.

High wages do not depend upon high prices of goods, nor low wages upon low prices. High and low wages depend upon the small or great number of labourers. There cannot be a glut of capital.

VIII.—KINDS OF CAPITAL.

THERE are two kinds of capital,—**circulating** and **fixed**. All kinds of capital are used in producing goods and services. Some, however, are used up by producing services or goods only once. Others repeat the same service over and over again. The money paid weekly or daily to the workmen who build a house is spent in food and clothing, and can do no more service to the capitalist. So the lime, wood, and stone are all used upon one house; but the tools with which the house is built will serve afterwards to build other houses. The reserve of a week's food, which the Indian made while building the canoe, was capital which was all consumed in producing it; but the canoe itself forms capital of a kind which may be used many a time in bringing home his game. The raw cotton is all gone when cloth is produced; the cotton-mill and machinery remain to turn other raw cotton into cloth. The seed of the farmer is gone, as well as the wages of his labourers, by the time when the next crop comes in; but his ploughs, and harrows, and barns remain to raise and house other crops.

Capital which is absorbed by being used only once, is called **circulating**; that which can be repeatedly used in production, is called **fixed capital**. All capital which, in being used once, completely changes its form, or its owner, is circulating capital. Thus the money paid to the labourer changes its owner, and the seed of the farmer changes its form. All capital which changes neither owner nor form, before yielding repeated services, or producing goods repeatedly, is fixed capital. Such are canoes and ploughs.

It is of great importance to labourers whether capital be fixed or circulating, since that which is fixed does not go to pay wages. Hence, if circulating capital is changed into fixed, the wages fund is reduced, and, of course, wages fall. When a railway is made, for example, much of the capital which was formerly circulating is made into fixed capital. Before it was made, the capital which has been employed in making it was used to pay wages to carriers, coach-drivers, ostlers, inn-servants, and many others. Now, the railway does their work. The capital is still in existence as an instrument for the conveyance of passengers and goods, which is not destroyed at each act of service, as the wages paid to these men for each act had been. Thus it is an evil to the labouring class when circulating is changed into fixed capital; and wages are, as it were, locked up from them. We shall soon see that, after a time, this very change increases the quantity of circulating capital, and, therefore, in the end, raises wages. But it does not do so at once, and, till the time comes, workmen are exposed to want.

The purpose of converting circulating into fixed capital is to make nature do our work, instead of labourers; for, as we know, nature requires no payment. The Indian turns his circulating capital of a week's provisions into the fixed capital of a canoe, because, by means of the canoe, water can be made to hold him up, and carry him easily to and from his hunting-ground; and the water does its work for nothing. In the same way, nature offers for nothing thousands of services to men, if they will only provide instruments by which they may receive the services. Let a man but enclose ground and prepare it a little, she will send heat, and light, and rain to make his seed grow for him; let him but put up a sail in his boat, and her winds will drive it for him, saving the expense of oarsmen; let him but dig a canal, she carries his goods along it by the upholding power of water; let him but make cylinders, and pistons, and wheels properly, she works them for him by the powers shut up in coal and iron, saving the toil of many workmen; let him but put a few plates of metal together in a sour liquid, and join them by wires as long as would go round the world, she gives him then the powers of the magnetic current, and sends his messages from hemisphere to hemisphere. When such instruments are made, circulating capital is turned into fixed, and nature does what labourers were previously paid to do. Their services are now less in demand, and, of course, their wages fall.

The question is often asked, "Can capitalists fix the rate of wages as they please?" and one now and then hears people speak as if they thought that capitalists both could and did do so. But neither capitalists nor labourers have it in their power to fix wages, unless it were possible for them to keep the population and the so-called wage fund always the same. Nor could a law passed by government do so; although many times such a thing has been attempted by law. Of course, if capitalists had all the power of making laws, they would wish to fix wages at a low rate; and if labourers had the sole power, they would fix them at a high rate. Now, let us see what a fixed wage means, and let us suppose that a government under the influence of capitalists had ordered that no workman should be paid more than fifteen shillings a week. Labour, as we know, is like everything else, bought and paid for according to what the purchaser thinks it worth, and what he can get it for. If, therefore, a man has occasion to purchase any kind of labour which he thinks worth thirty shillings a week, because of the trouble it would save him, and knows that he could not get it for less if the law did not compel people to work for him, such a law means that he must not pay so much. He must buy for fifteen shillings what he knows to be worth thirty.

Or, suppose that a kindly government, pitying the underpaid labourer, were to pass a law ordering that all labourers must be paid thirty shillings a week. In that case a man must pay thirty shillings for work which he knows, it may be, to be only worth fifteen. The injustice of such laws it is easy to see. And they can never be maintained in any country. Skilled workmen, whose wages are made too low by law, and fixed at a rate as high for those who are unskilled as for them, would cease to work, or at least would cease to work efficiently; and their masters would be compelled to bribe them secretly with a high wage contrary to law, or would lose in the kind of work done more than they gained by a law fixing wages low.

On the other hand, if workmen are paid too high, by the law fixing a high rate for all, then the capitalists who have saved, in order to employ labour, feeling that they have to pay too high for it, will no longer think it worth while to save. The wage fund will decrease, and if such a system of fixed high payments for all, skilful and unskilful workmen alike, continues—whether it continue by force of law, or by any other force which workmen may have—men would soon cease to save anything, and in the end there would be no work for any one, for there would be no capital to pay wages.

The railways and steamships and electric wires of modern times give capital a means of escaping from the effects of such laws before it is entirely destroyed. The man who finds that his capital is taken away unjustly, by law or by any other means, or that he does not receive so high a reward for the use of his savings in one country as in another, will, and can easily, take them to that other. A hundred years ago no British merchants had places of business in other parts of Europe than their own land—now many have; and if any attempts to fix wages at too high a rate for capital to receive its due share in the rewards of production were successful here, doubtless capital would take refuge abroad; and the effects of such attempts would be that workmen would be left at last without the means of earning wages.

Circulating capital is that kind which changes its owner or its form in rendering services, and renders them only once.

Fixed capital is that which does not change its owner or its form in rendering services, and renders them repeatedly.

By means of fixed capital the services of the forces of nature are secured.

Capitalists cannot fix the rate of wages, and laws to do so are either useless or hurtful.

IX.—PROFITS.

We have seen that in the production of wealth three things combine—*First*, Nature, who furnishes the properties of air, of water, of coal, of the soil, of heat, light, and magnetism; *second*, Labour; and, *third*, Capital, which is only a mode of labour, since it is the share taken in production by the savings of what former labour earned. Nature requires no pay, the workmen get wages, the reward of capital is called profit. It is evident that the capitalist must obtain some reward for his services. If he did not furnish the tools and materials and wages, goods could not be produced; and, certainly, if he got nothing, he would not furnish them.

Suppose that, as in the case of the housebuilders we spoke of before, he give tools, stone, and lime; and does, in addition, his share of the work. For his work he must receive wages like the other workmen. But he also pays the workmen their wages as the work goes on. They get their share of the price of the house without any doubt, whereas he runs the risk of losing both his materials, the wages he has paid them, and his own wages, should any accident occur to the building—its foundation turn out to be bad, or the person for whom it is being built turn out unable to pay for it. He must therefore be paid for the risk he runs of losing all.

Besides, and this is an important matter, he might have chosen not to give these wages and tools and materials in advance, and have used them or the money which furnished them on his own pleasure. He will therefore require to be paid, because he has abstained from pleasure which he might have enjoyed. If not, why should he abstain? and if he did not abstain, where would be the capital? These three things then go to form the share of a capitalist in the final price of goods—*First*,

His own wage; *second*, Payment for risk; and, *third*, Payment for abstinence.

His wages will rise and fall like the wages of other labourers. If his share of the work be of a kind which many can do, and few want, they will be small; and, if of a kind which few can do and many want, they will be large. Therefore, in judging how the capitalist's share of the price of produce rises and falls differently from that of the labourer, we must consider how the amounts which he gets for risk and abstinence rise and fall. For this reason it will be better to think of the capitalist as one who takes no share in the labour of producing the goods out of which his share comes, but who takes the risk in regard to the price being paid at last, and furnishes in advance the wages and the material, or, what is the same thing, money enough for both wages and material.

1. Risk.—Let us suppose that the price of the finished goods will not be finally paid before a year after the materials, tools, and wages are advanced. At the end of that year the capitalist will naturally expect to get all the money that he has advanced restored to him, and something more as the payment for his abstinence. But the workmen may be dishonest, or the goods may turn out to be of a kind which few or none want. Or the money may have been advanced not to produce goods, but to send out ships for foreign goods, such as corn from Odessa; and the corn may get wet and spoil, or the ship may be wrecked. Such risks as these a capitalist runs every time he advances money; he may lose all, both his savings and their reward, or he may lose only a part. A man will naturally lend his money, or advance capital for a much smaller profit when he is certain of receiving both his capital and the reward, than when he is uncertain; and the greater the uncertainty or risk, the more he will demand. A capitalist will require large profits when he advances money to a shopkeeper whose honour is suspected, and not so much from any one who is known to be thoroughly honest and able to conduct business well. Governments which are known to have borrowed

from capitalists and refused to pay, find that, in all future attempts to obtain advances of money, capitalists demand large profits for the risk they run. When a government borrows money, the security against risk which they offer to lenders, is the taxes which the people under it will pay in future years. But sometimes, when a change of rulers occurs, the new rulers refuse to pay the money which has been borrowed by the old ones. This is called repudiating their national debts. The British Government alone, of all those in Europe, has never repudiated its debts; and the consequence is that capitalists will advance money to it, for a smaller profit than to any other government. They run, it may be said, no risk at all in making such advances.

2. **Abstinence.**—When no risk is run, and no part of the labour of producing goods is taken by the capitalist, then the sole element of his profit is payment for abstinence. This payment is called **interest**; so that while profit, strictly speaking, is a mixed payment for labour, risk, and abstinence, interest is payment for abstinence alone. Some people say that payments for merely refraining from the use of money should never be made. "Why," say they, "should money make money? If you put a hundred sovereigns into a bag, will you find a hundred and five in it at the end of a year? Or, if you put twenty gold watches into it, will you find twenty-one when the twelve months are over?" But that there must and ought to be some payment, even when there is no risk, no one, on a fair consideration, will deny. If one man were to say to another, " Give me twenty shillings, and I will give you a pound," no exchange of services could be fairer, for each of these sums represents the same value in other goods. But suppose that on its having been agreed to, the first, before the exchange is made, should say, " I mean you to give me the twenty shillings now, and I will give you the pound a year hence." Is not the case altered? Should the giver of the twenty shillings dispense for a whole year with the use of all he could buy with them, and give them to another man so

long for nothing? As an act of friendship, perhaps he might—or of charity; but, in society, the foundation of which is service for service, such an exchange cannot be.

Money which is lent to the British Government is sure always to be repaid ; and hence the rate of interest paid by that government tells us what at any time is the reward which capitalists receive for abstinence alone. When we say that the debts of the British Government are always paid, we must be understood with regard to the yearly interest of these debts. Let us explain this a little more fully.

During the many wars of which our history tells us, vast sums have been borrowed by the Government, mostly from British capitalists. The interest has always been paid; the sum originally lent is not required to be repaid, for the lender receives the right to receive the interest yearly till it is repaid; and if at any time he tires of getting merely interest, he can sell his right to it, and he will, at any time, receive for that right a sum nearly equal in value to the sum originally lent. People who hold the right to the interest are said to have property in the **Funds**, or in the **Stocks**; the agents who arrange for buying and selling the right are called **Stockbrokers**; and the place where the right is sold is called the **Stock Exchange**. Property in the Funds, like every other kind of goods, rises and falls in value according as many wish to sell it, and few to buy it, or the reverse.

Just as a man may acquire a right to yearly payments of interest from Government, so he may acquire a right to yearly payments of the profits of any business which is carried on by others, or by himself with others. Any number of men may agree to join portions of their capital together to make a railway, it may be, or to found a bank, or perhaps to bring water into a city. Such a company is called a **Joint-Stock Company**. The whole sum needed to do the work is divided into shares, and each man advances a certain sum of money, say a hundred pounds, upon every share that he agrees to take. According to his shares, or his stock, as they are called, will be his part of the profits. When a man is tired of merely receiving profits, he can sell his shares; and, if the company's business be successful, he may get more than a hundred pounds for each share; or, if it be not successful, he will get less. They rise and fall in value like Government Stock, and all other property. Stockbrokers are the agents for buying and selling such shares.

There are men who make it their business to buy stock in home and foreign funds, and shares in railway and other stock, when they are low in price, and to sell them when they rise. Such men are called **Speculators**, and some think they are hurtful members of society. Their trade is looked upon as a kind of gambling. But, if I held stock, let us say in the funds of Peru, or of any other foreign government, and thought that probably the next yearly interest would not be paid because a revolution had occurred in Peru, naturally I should wish to sell such stock. It is surely good for me, in such a case, that I can find a speculator who will buy it, and run the risk of loss. And suppose that every other who held Peruvian stock should wish also to sell it, then, if there were no speculators, we should all be anxious to sell, and no one to buy, and the result would be that our stock would become worthless. These speculators save us from heavy loss, and keep the prices of stock more equal, by supplying it when it is dear, and buying it up when it is cheap. There is hardly any evil in trade worse than ups and downs in price, or fluctuations; and speculators help to prevent these. Of course, the men who spread lies about revolutions and dangers, to make funds fall in value and buy them cheap, deserve to be condemned and punished, like all other seekers of gain by foul means. Such are often spoken of as "bears;" and those who rush to sell their stock in needless fear and haste, as "bulls." But, so long as speculators buy and sell shares, aiming to make profit by the ordinary changes in supply and demand of stock, they render a service to society.

There are also speculators in corn against whom many have strong prejudices. These buy corn when it is cheap, and sell it when it is dear. It is said that they make the food of the poor man dear. In times of scarcity their warehouses have been broken into and plundered, and few pitied them. Let us look at what they do. Certainly they seek profit like every other trader, but they only get it by rendering service. If, when corn were cheap, everybody got it and used it plentifully, then, in years when crops were bad, little or none could be had. These men buy it up when it is cheap, store it away, and keep it from being wasted. It is true, that by buying it they make it somewhat dearer in cheap years; but then, when a year of famine comes, the corn is sold at a price which yields them a high profit; but still at a price much lower than it would have been, had they not stored it up. They earn their profits then by rendering a most important service.

A capitalist's profits consist of payment of his wages, risk, and abstinence.

A fundholder is one who possesses a right to be paid yearly the interest of money lent to Government.

Speculators in the funds, and in shares of joint-stock companies, or in corn render an important service to society. They prevent excessive fluctuations in the prices of funds, and shares, and corn.

X.—INTEREST.

To lend the use of money is the same in effect as to lend the use of goods. For money, while it measures goods, represents them, as we have said; that is, it serves as a mark of a right which he who holds it has to receive a certain amount of goods and services for it. If I possess half-a-sovereign, that means that in some way I have given goods or services to society, for which society owes me a certain amount of services in return. When I spend it,

I give it to some one who gives me goods or services; and as he now holds it, he has the right to others in return. Thus to lend money is to lend goods or services. But there need not be as much money in a country as there are goods. For since money is only a measure of goods, men have no more need of a pound in money for every pound's worth of goods, than they have of a separate footrule for every foot of land or timber which they possess.

The merchants of Great Britain lend in a single week probably three hundred millions of pounds, while there is not above one-fifth part of so much coin in the whole country, and more than the half of that part is shut up in the stores of the Bank of England. How then could they lend three hundred millions with at the most twenty millions? Only by really lending their capital—the goods which they have saved. If, then, a farmer were to lend another a hundred bushels of corn, and should receive at the end of a year a hundred bushels, and a reward for his abstinence of five more, the transaction is of the same nature exactly as when a capitalist lends money to a producer of goods, and receives after a given time his money back with interest. Indeed, people do part with the use of goods for a time, and receive again both the goods and a reward for their abstinence. This reward is of the same nature as interest, but is called by another name. Men lend ships for a voyage, what they receive in payment is called **freight;** and horses and cabs when lent bring in a reward called **hire.** Men lend houses to others to dwell in, or to trade in, and their reward is called **rent.** Now, if many men have a large number of horses which they are anxious to lend, and few people wish to borrow them, the rate of hire for horses cannot be high. For, if there be two men each with a horse to lend, and only one with a desire to borrow, he will take the horse of the man who will lend it him for the lowest hire. So if there be many farms to let, or houses, and few people who wish them, rents will be low.

Since the lending of money is of the same nature as

the lending of horses, or houses, or ships, its payment is also of the same nature, and thus interest will rise or fall according to the same law as rent, hire, or freight. If there be many willing to lend money, and few trustworthy borrowers, the rate of interest is low; if there be few lenders and many borrowers, it is high. We see, thus, that the consideration of "how many offer any service, and how many demand it," runs through all we learn in political economy; in fact, we begin to find by this time that while society is founded on the law of "Service for service," the value of services is founded on the law of supply and demand. The rewards of labour and capital, of risk and abstinence, wages, profits, rent, hire, freight, and interest, all vary according to this law.

The capitalists of Holland receive smaller interest from their government than the capitalists of Great Britain from theirs; the first receive about two, the others three pounds for every hundred lent. The reason is that the Dutch are a saving people. Those among them who have money to lend are many; those who wish to borrow are few; hence interest is low.

Thus we see how a difference in the character of a people may make the supply of a special kind of service differ, or the demand differ; but the law remains ever true, that "a great supply and small demand lowers the value of a service,—a small supply and great demand raises it." If the British people saved more, the rate of interest would fall in this country. Other circumstances, besides increased or diminished savings, alter the relations of the supply of, and the demand for, money. In Australia, lenders receive six per cent. from government, and more from farmers, because there is risk to run, as well as abstinence, in lending to them. But the farmers there are willing to pay high interest, for the land is fertile, and population increasing; and hence profits as a whole are large. The demand for money to enclose and cultivate more land is therefore great, and the supply of capital is small in relation to it.

The capitalist does not always wait to the end of the year before he gets the reward of his abstinence in the shape of interest. He most frequently, as he is in the act of lending the money,—say a hundred pounds, at five per cent.,—takes off his interest at once, and pays to the borrower only ninety-five pounds. Of course, he expects to get his hundred pounds at the end of a year. The reward of abstinence in this form is called discount. It is the same as interest in every respect, except in the time of payment. Yet there is a striking difference in the variations of the rates of interest and discount. The rate of interest, without payment for risk, has been nearly the same for many years to the British capitalist—about three per cent.; the rate of discount changes many times in a year, and may vary in amount from two to ten pounds per hundred. It is hard to explain the causes of this. The chief one is, that those who borrow and pay for the loan by discount are needy, and there is risk in lending to them. They are usually people who borrow only for a short time, perhaps to get some passing chance in trade. Discount will vary, therefore, with every occasional change in the quantity of capital, and in the number of borrowers. Interest is paid on loans for long periods; it is, therefore, less altered by merely temporary changes, and so remains steadily at a more fixed rate, above and below which discount sways continually.

Can there be two different rates of interest in the same country at the same time? No; if interest be taken, as it should always be, to mean payment for abstinence, where no risk is run and no labour done. For nobody will give away the use of his money for a less reward than others receive. A capitalist will cease to lend to those who give least interest, and lend it only to those who give most. As every lender will do the same, and all will try to get the highest payment for abstinence which can be had, it is easy to see that all interest will, in the end, rise or fall to the same level, according as more or less money is offered for loan.

There may, however, be very different rates of profit in

different trades, in the same country, and at the same time. For profit is payment for abstinence, and for risk, and for labour which the man who advances money in a trade usually gives by superintending and directing the work of the other labourers. Now, different trades have very different risks, according to the kind of goods or services produced; and, also, the superintendence of the production of different kinds of goods requires very different kinds of skill; and, besides, trades differ in being agreeable or disagreeable. The part of payment of profits which arises from interest will be always the same in all trades of a country; but the payments for risk and superintendence will thus differ greatly. In the same trade, however, the profits will always be the same at the same time, just as interest is always the same at the same time in the trade of lending money without risk.

Very high interest is often called **usury**; and those who require it, before they will lend, are called **usurers**. In using terms properly, interest means the price of money when there is no risk of loss, usury when there is great risk. If men run the risk of lending money to the very needy, or the dishonest, or the profligate, they must have interest which amounts to usury, in order that their gains, when they do gain, may make up for their losses, which must be frequent. For if they are not, then the risk cannot be great. The taking of interest, or usury as it is called, from each other was forbidden to the Jews. Their great lawgiver, Moses, sought to teach them to be kindly to each other, and probably they were not without need of the lesson. They were allowed, however, to take it from those who were not Jews. Our own government in old times passed laws forbidding and punishing usury, and such laws existed in Italy and Prussia till recent times. Their object was to save poor borrowers from the greed of money-lenders; but such an object cannot be gained by forbidding high rates of interest. The punishment for breaking the law is, in fact, made into a new risk which the lender must run if he consents to lend; and thus the poor man can either not borrow at all, or he has to pay still higher usury for this extra risk. Such laws are rarely proposed now, although sometimes ignorant people wish government to fix, by law, a rate of discount which may not be exceeded without a penalty. Such people forget that there is no way of fixing the amount of discount or interest, but by fixing the amount of all the capital which may be saved, and of all the money that people must try to borrow.

To lend money is the same as to give the use of goods for a time. Interest, hire, freight, and rent, are all payments for abstinence; and their amount is fixed by the law of supply and demand.

Usury is interest where great risk is run. It is not, in itself, unjust; and to forbid it by law is hurtful to borrowers.

XI.—MACHINERY.

SINCE all wealth is produced by **nature, capital,** and **labour,** it is clear that the more nature can be made to do, the less will be required from capital and labour. If nature can, by any means, be made to bring about services which before needed the combined efforts of the other two, then these two will be set free to bring about new services, and mankind will be the gainers.

When men invent **machines,** they make instruments by which nature is brought to do work. The advantage is evident; for we know that labour and capital require pay, but nature does not.

Tools are machines of a simple kind, by means of which nature works for us; but it is in the more complex machines, such as the steam-engine, that we see best how she can be made to serve us. In fact, scarcely any kind of service is ever done by a man to himself, or to his neighbours, without the help of some kind of tool or machinery. The savage, who cannot mount the bare-stemmed cocoa-nut tree, ties a stone to a piece of string formed by the twining fibres of a climbing plant, flings it over the branch, and brings the nut down. He breaks the nut, after he has got it, by letting a heavy stone fall upon it; and he gets to his hunting-ground by means of his canoe. The string, the stone, the canoe, are all machines which give him the use of the forces of nature; and so, to us, are knives, wheelbarrows, ships, railways, electric telegraphs, and printing-presses; and, in fact, everything with which men do work, over and above their hands, feet, and teeth. The more machines there are in the world, and the better they are, the richer men must be, and the abler to live easily; for nature does their work. The man, therefore, who invents a new machine renders a great service to his fellow-men.

And yet there are many men who can say, and say truly, that new machines have been no blessing to them. Here is one breaking stones upon the roadside, and earning about twelve shillings a week. Not many years ago he was a calico printer,—that is, he used to put the pretty patterns on calico dresses by means of blocks of wood, which were first dipped into a sieve containing colouring matter, and then laid on to the spread-out cloth. He could earn at that trade two pounds a week. But a machine in the form of a cylinder was invented, which puts the colours on the cloth much better and quicker than he could with his hands and block. Nature does this work now; and, as capital and labour have had only their ordinary reward, we, society, get the benefit of her work in cheaper and prettier dresses than before. Our mothers, and sisters, and wives can, for very little, have a dress such as only a duchess could afford to buy in the olden time. But this poor man's work is no longer needed, and he can earn no wage now, except that miserable pittance which he gets for road-mending. Let us sit down beside him, in imagination, and talk with him about machines and inventions.

"I wish they were all at the bottom of the sea," he

says; "they take away the poor man's work and wages." So they do, you may admit, and then ask him if he really means all machines. "Do you also mean printing-blocks and colour-sieves?" He will tell you no, but only such as the printing cylinder. "Did the blocks and sieves print better and cheaper than cylinders?" you may ask; and he will allow that they did not. Then you may easily show him that he and the enemies of machinery wish only that the more perfect machines should be destroyed, and the imperfect ones retained.

Next you may show him that though they take away work at first, they afterwards cause more employment than before. "For instance," you may say, "before book printing was invented, a few men made good wages by copying books in hand-writing. These lost their work when books began to be printed; but now, instead of a few writers, see the immense number of type-setters, bookbinders, papermakers, newsboys, and others who are employed in connection with the printing press. Again, about a hundred years ago, the cotton manufacturers employed only some forty thousand persons at about five shillings a week each. Now, since machinery has been invented, above two millions are employed in one way or another in cotton mills, and the average wage is about a pound a week. Yet again, when railways were first proposed, men thought with pity upon all the coach-drivers, ostlers, innkeepers, and others who were likely to be thrown out of employment, and who, indeed, were thrown out of it; but they did not foresee the enormous traffic that was to come instead; the inns, larger and more of them; the horses and coachmen more numerous and better paid than ever, who ply their trade at railway stations; the loads of goods that pass between these stations and the warehouses in manufacturing towns; the clerks in railway offices, the guards, the drivers, the porters; the hosts, in fact, of railway employees, as it is now the fashion to call them."

Again, you may show him that machines not only give employment to far more than were employed before, in connection with them indirectly; but they give employment to large numbers who before had no such employment in the making of machinery itself. "Yes! machines increase the demand for labour, and so increase the wages of the labourers."

It will be easy next to show that machines cheapen the comforts of life, and enable the poor to get them as well as the rich. You can speak to him of the halfpenny and the penny newspaper, and compare them with the price of books when men wrote instead of printing them; and may show him, too, how the cheapness of goods leads many to buy them, increases the demand for them, and causes a demand for labour to supply them.

Again, you may lead him to see that machines not only enable us to do things quicker, and better, and cheaper than before, but they enable men to do things that, without them, would have been quite impossible. "How," you may ask, "could the ocean be crossed without ships? How could the water be got out of mines without pumps? How could men speak to those on the other side of the world, and receive answers almost immediately, without the electric telegraph?"

And remembering always that it is only the more perfect machines he complains of, and that he wishes to retain those that are less perfect, you may ask, "Is it no advantage to the labouring man that his strength should be spared by the use of machinery? Was it no advantage to those whose arms were stiff and sore by rowing in the galleys of ancient times, that first sails, and then steamships with paddles and screws were invented? Was it no advantage to those who ground corn by rubbing it between heavy stones, that the wind-mill and the water-mill were invented? Yes, hard bodily spirit-crushing labour is done away with by machinery, and men are left free to become what they should be—thinking beings."

But, say what you like, the displaced working man shakes his head. "They increase the demand for labour, do they?" he says. "Has the printing drum increased the demand for *my* labour? that's what I want to know. Don't tell me that larger numbers than before are better employed than ever. Am *I* better employed? Where are *my* increased wages?"

And, really, it is impossible to give *him* a satisfactory answer. Before actual suffering it is sometimes better to be silent. For the truth is, every new invention brings about a change, and in all changes some one must suffer. The good of machinery is that though, at first, it causes a few to suffer, in the end it spreads enjoyment and comfort over a very much larger number. He will never feel that, and at his age it would be only cruelty to tell him of what is, perhaps, the only remedy; this namely, that the working man in his youth should strive after a good education; for then, whatever be his trade, if new machinery turns him out of work at it, he will be able readily to change to work that may pay him even better than the old.

There are cases where machinery does not necessarily increase the demand for the goods which it makes cheaper. Suppose that everybody had a hat already, a machine for making hats would not make them want more. Or if hearses could be made more easily by new machinery, would more be bought in any town, which was not increasing in population? No more faces of clocks and watches could be bought however they might be cheapened, unless at the same time another machine cheapened the inside works. Yet even in such cases invention causes an increased demand for labour and a rise of wages.

A hatter can make as many hats as his customers require by means of two workmen to whom he pays a hundred pounds in wages. He gets a machine, however, by means of which he can produce the same number of hats with only one workman. Now his customers require no more hats than he used to make. What else can he do but dismiss one workman, and produce his hats for fifty pounds? What then comes of the other fifty? Our hatter is a business man, and knows better than to spend it, or let it lie idle. He, therefore, puts it into another branch of business. It remains capital as before, and gives employment to labour as before. There is no difference made in the capital seeking labour, nor in the labour seeking capital to employ it. There is this difference, however, one working man requires to cease from making hats, and to go with his labour to a new branch of trade.

But that is not all. Hats must become cheaper. Other hat makers will also get machines, which produce hats for half the money. Their profits are now great, but they will all be anxious to sell, and as no more hats are needed in the town, each will try to increase his custom by giving up a little of his large profit, and selling cheaper than the others; and one sells below another, for the same reason, till at last they have all given up their extra profits from the machine. Now who gets the benefit of the saving in labour which the machine has effected? The hat buyers. And what then? They save more money than they could before; this is added to the capital of the country, and gives employment to additional labour. Thus even when there is no increased demand for the goods which a machine cheapens, there is an increase of capital and more labour employed. The only evil is that some workmen have required to change their trade, and that will be no great evil supposing they are educated, and can easily learn a new one.

This world is full of hindrances to our comforts and our pleasures. Machinery helps to remove these hindrances. I am hungry; and there is plenty of corn lying at Odessa. The distance is the hindrance to my getting food; and ships remove that. I am cold. The hindrance to my being warmed is that wool and cotton do not grow in the shape of coats and shirts, and that coals lie deep underground. Spinning-machines, and steam-looms, and miners' tools remove that. I want to see my friends. The hindrance is the long and rough roads that lie between them and me. Railways remove that. Why should we not bless machines,—we human beings that are liable to hunger and cold, and whose bosoms warm with friendship and love?

Machines make nature do work for us. They displace labour at first, but afterwards cause a much greater demand for it than existed before their invention. They give employment to people in the making of them. They enable us to do things quicker and better, and what, without them, would be impossible. They save a waste of human strength. They create a demand for labour even when the quantity of goods they make is not increased.

XII.—THRIFT AND SPENDTHRIFT.

CAPITAL is saving, but not hoarding. It is spending, but only with a view to the production of future goods and services. Let us henceforth use the word **commodities** to mean goods and services. There is a saving, then, which is not capital; and a laying out which produces no new commodities. The miser, who lays his gold in bags, and boxes, and nooks of garrets, only that he may gloat over it at night, is no capitalist; nor yet is he who has plenty of money, but spends it in wine, fine linen, horse-racing, and the like. We all hate a miser, and with reason; his savings do no good to himself or to any other while he lives. But, somehow, a prodigal is often looked upon by the world as a fine fellow. "He spends his money, and encourages trade," people say. "If he smashes windows in jest, and pays for them, it is good for glaziers; if, in a frolic, he turns over his carriage, and breaks the shafts and springs, it is good for the coachmakers. He is kind-hearted, makes money circulate, and is nobody's enemy but his own." Now, if this were true, then the best thing for trade would be to go on destroying. To burn London would be a fine thing for masons and carpenters; and general destruction of all things would cause a general good trade.

Another man, not a miser, but one who uses his money well, who employs it as capital, for the production of useful things which come back to him with yearly profits, —a man who looks strictly to his business, and never wastes,—he is not half so well liked by his neighbours. Now, the question is, which of these two men does best for these neighbours? Which of them encourages trade most? Let us see. The prodigal spends his year's income in champagne and gloves, hires cabs, and has a box at the opera. Good! he has caused work to some, and no doubt sent the money into the pockets of shopkeepers, cab-hirers, theatre proprietors, and the rest. That money may be used by them rightly or wrongly; but, when the gloves are faded, the cabs gone home, and the opera past, what has he left out of his year's income to help workmen with? And the short demand for commodities which his extravagance caused ends there; the commodities are gone, and he can employ no more labour. Thus a demand for commodities is not a demand for labour; indeed, would end in the destruction of all means of support for labour, if everybody were like the prodigal.

The other, who uses his money well, lays it out, let us say, in draining fields, building houses, or in the purchase of railway stock. He, too, makes money circulate as plentifully as the prodigal; for it goes into the pockets of drain-makers, builders, and railway employees. That money may be used rightly or wrongly by them; but, at the year's end, what is his position? He gets a larger crop from the fields; he gets rent for the houses which have sheltered tenants for the year; he gets payment of profit from the railway; and, if not exactly in a year, some time sooner or later, he gets all his money back again, increased by the profits to which his abstinence has given him a right. He has it all, and more, again to spend in useful labours, and to put once more into the pockets of workmen. And the same thing is repeated every time his money comes back to him with profits.

Which, then, is the best for his neighbours—the prodigal or the money-maker? Follow the prodigal's career, after his fortune is gone, and perhaps you find him a beggar, or a burden on his friends; the other is every year able to pay more and more to labourers.

Let working men continue to dislike misers, who are so ignorant and infatuated as to take money for what it only represents; but let them also learn to judge correctly regarding prodigality and luxury. For by luxury is meant spending of money upon that which leads to no use or profit.

What then, it may be asked, shall there be no seeking of harmless pleasure, because political economy has pointed out the virtue of capital and the duty of saving? Are we to do away with coachmakers, glovemakers, importers of champagne and other wines, with opera singers and all others whose services are merely sources of pleasure, the money paid for which does not come back to us every time it is laid out with profit? So far from saying any such thing, political economy is the study of how to increase human comforts, how to remove obstacles in the way of convenience and reasonable pleasure. Does it not approve of machinery, because that lessens our trouble and increases the number of commodities? There is a kind of luxury which refines the tastes, relieves the mind from the oppression of over-work, and increases the productive powers of those who enjoy it; and the best arguments of the science are drawn from the fact that, as its truths are acted upon society advances, our comforts increase, and things which were the expensive luxuries of former times become the every-day enjoyments of life. Were nothing but what is needful for work allowable, then we should drink only water, eat black bread like the ancient Spartans, and wear the coarsest stuffs. The time was when men slept on bare boards, and ate from wooden dishes; when chimneys were looked upon as mere refinements; when glass windows, forks, coffee, tea, feather pillows, were all condemned by severe men who strove to keep up the hardiness of their race. Yet, as progress goes on, these have all come into common use, and mankind are better and stronger and more able to produce commodities because of them. Only such pleasures are blameable as are bought either at the expense of future wants, or by the neglect of what we owe to others.

* All ornament is luxury of a kind—churches, picture galleries, flower gardens, public parks, and the like; but political economy says clearly that evil would ensue were such things not made and enjoyed; for those whose labour is absorbed by them would then be forced to strive for other labour, and would reduce the wages of those who were engaged in plainer work.

In fact, it will be well for the working man when a certain measure of what is called luxury becomes a necessity for him; when he will not think life worth having, or work worth doing, unless, as a result of it, his home be neat and rightly furnished, unless his rooms be large enough and sufficient in number and well papered, his book-shelves well filled with the works of the best writers, his wife well dressed, his children well taught, and his and their food always wholesome in quality and enough in quantity. When men will refuse to work unless such things can be gained, and when education has given them minds which will regard such things, not as luxuries, but as things needful; when no man will think of marrying until he can provide them for his family by what he has saved and what he can earn; when, thus, the land will not be crowded with too many ill-fed, ill-taught children, who grow up to strive as workmen against each other, and so reduce wages, then wages must rise, and the love of luxury within proper limits will be the very instrument that has made them rise.

Woe to the nation whose workmen, no matter through what cause, have no higher needs than hunger and thirst, and are content with a clothing of rags and houses of mud!

And, indeed, it should not be said that this is the only advantage to be gained from the outlay of money upon pictures, sculpture, and ornament of different kinds, that they refine the tastes, and help to elevate the character, and through that the condition of a nation. They may also become a source of profit even in a commercial point of view. In the Netherlands are many galleries, on the walls of which hang hundreds of works of the greatest artists. There they have hung for a century or two. They were bought in days when the merchants of Belgium were very rich, it may be to gratify their taste and their pride. But time has made them of immense value, and were they now sold they would bring many times the prices that were first paid for them. They form, thus, a kind of **fixed capital** on the walls of the museums and galleries of Antwerp, Brussels, and the Hague.

Neither the miser nor the prodigal are useful members of society. What the prodigal spends destroys the results of labour, and does not create a demand for it.

Luxury which refines the taste and strengthens the love of intellectual pursuits, and is not inconsistent with duty, is perfectly justifiable. A certain amount of habitual luxury is a means of raising wages.

XIII.—PRICE.

ALL the **services** of all who have helped to produce any **commodity** must be paid for, when it is bought to be consumed or used—the wages of the workmen who made it, or any part of it, and the abstinence of the men by whose capital any part of it was enabled to be produced. For what would happen if these wages and profits were not paid in the loaf that one buys? The baker would not continue to bake loaves if he were not paid; neither would the miller continue to grind the wheat, nor the farmer to plough and sow and reap and lend his capital for wages to farm servants. Of course we do not mean paid by that one loaf, but partly by it, and wholly by the price of all the wheat and other things got from his land. In the same way the miner would cease to dig iron for ploughs, unless the part paid by the flour in this loaf, and by all the other produce raised by all the ploughs for which he found the iron, were sufficient to reward his services. So we may go backwards, and we shall find that whenever a workman whose work was needful, or a capitalist whose savings were needful to furnish any commodity, was not sufficiently paid, that workman or that capitalist would withdraw his services, and the commodity would no longer be produced. All these payments make up the cost of production, and thus we may see that the lowest price for which any commodity can be regularly sold in the market is the amount of the cost of production. It is true, that after goods have been produced—a book, a loaf, or anything else—we may buy them at times for less than the cost of production; but that can only be because some of the producers have made a mistake, and given their services in producing a commodity which no one desires so much that he will pay the natural price for it. The cost of production is called the **natural price**; the **market price** is either just a little above or just a little below it. But when a producer has made the mistake once, and finds that he cannot get the cost of production, he will take care not to repeat it, and the commodity will cease to be produced.

There are three modes in which commodities differ as to the quantity of them which can be brought into the market.

First, Some kinds of goods cannot be produced again by any quantity of labour or capital. Pictures by Raphael or Wilkie cannot, since Raphael and Wilkie are dead; neither can coins of the Emperor Tiberius, nor wines of last year's growth. The supply of such things can by no means be increased.

Second, Some goods require more labour to produce a given quantity, if more of them be wanted. The cost of production is increased, and therefore their prices must rise. The more corn men want, fields must be dug that are farther from markets, or poorer in soil, than those cultivated before; the more iron and coal men want, the deeper into mines they must go; the more fish men want, the farther fishermen must go out with their nets and lines. All sorts of food and of minerals and raw materials belong to this division.

Third, Some goods are of such a nature that the more the world wants of them the less is their cost of production, and therefore the cheaper they can be sold. Pocket-handkerchiefs, shawls, cottons, linens, in truth all manufactured goods, are of this third kind.

The market price of the first kind is altogether independent of the cost of production; that of the other two cannot be less than it, but is regulated by the **supply** of, and the **demand** for, them. The supply and demand must in one way or other be made equal in all three before we can tell what their market price is.

Were you ever at an auction sale, at which one picture by a famous old master, or a rare copy of some old book was to be sold? Then you can easily understand how the supply and demand are equalized in the price of goods of the first kind, those whose quantity cannot be increased in the market. Take, for example, a sale of rare books. See these six well dressed old gentlemen,—for somehow it is always well-to-do old gentlemen who want rare old books. Observe how they slily and doubtfully watch each other from under their six pairs of spectacles. All six are after one and the same old book, so rare, that it is said, no other copy of the same edition exists. The auctioneer puts it up. The bidding goes on. One bids freely till the price is £60, and then he stops; another bids till it is £70, then he stops; another bids on till it is £80, and then he stops. The other three bid on; one stops at £90; at £100 the fifth old gentleman stops; and gentleman number six smiles blandly, wiping his bald forehead, as the book is knocked down to him for £105. The supply one copy, and the demand one gentleman, have been made equal by a price of £105. At £60 the demand lessened by one; at £70 by two, and so on, till at last, at above £100, a demand of only one was left. Had the auctioneer pretended to hear a higher bid than £105, gentleman number six might have dropped off too, and there would have been no sale.

Of articles thus absolutely limited in supply, called articles of **monopoly**, or **single sale**, the price will always be higher the greater the demand, and may be raised up to the highest sum which any one will give, but not higher.

Now, in regard to articles of the second kind, the cost of production of which increases as the demand increases, the price of them will also be always higher the greater the demand. But the demand for them cannot be diminished by raising the price always higher and higher. They are mainly articles of food, and people cannot withdraw from demanding them; however high be the price they must have food. To bring the supply to an equality with the demand, the only way is to raise more corn and other farm produce. Fields that were left untilled before must be taken in, grain must be brought from a greater distance, new manures must be sought, anything done to increase the supply, for the demand cannot be diminished. When in this case will supply and demand be equal? When men by tilling fields at greater expense have produced corn enough to feed the people; and then the price of corn will rise till it suffices to pay the increased cost of production in the poorest fields which have to be cultivated.

Of course, corn will, as before, be got with ease out of the richer fields; but those who own these richer fields will get the benefit. For all the corn in the market will be of the same price, that of the cost of production in the poorest soil; and what is true of corn is true of any other article of agricultural produce, of all raw materials, and the produce of mines and fisheries.

Next, let us see how demand and supply are made equal in the case of manufactured goods. Although shawls, shirts, and gloves require a supply of the raw materials of which they are made, wool, linen, and leather, and come so far under the rule of agricultural produce, yet the raw material forms a very small part of the price of manufactured goods. By far the great part of their cost of production lies in payments for labour. How few are the workmen whose services are required in a cotton field, compared with those who are required from the time cotton leaves the plantation, till it enters the draper's shop a finished shirt! And the greater the quantity of manufactured goods required, on so much the larger scale can the manufacture be carried on. Division of labour can then be carried to a greater extent, and one foreman or overlooker can as easily superintend a department with two hundred, as with one hundred, workers. The cost of production will thus always be less, the greater the demand for such goods.

On what terms then will supply and demand be made equal in regard to manufactured goods? By the demand being such that the price given will pay the cost of production at least, and the supply such that the price is not much above the cost of production. How can this supply and demand be known? Who can tell how many hats, or shawls, or gloves will be wanted in any one week or year? The demand varies, and the supply must be made to vary with it. This is simply done. If manufacturers produce more gloves, for example, than there is a demand for,—that is, than can be sold at the cost of production, —there is what is called a glut in the market in regard to these goods. They lie unsold in the shops and warehouses, or have to be sold at less than the natural price. Care is then taken that no more be produced for a while; the supply becomes gradually less in proportion to the demand, and then the market price rises. The people who want gloves find that they must pay more in order to get a pair, and in the end the market price will rise sufficiently to pay the cost of production of the goods; for no more will be produced till it does.

It may happen that, with a given quantity of goods in the market, such prices are got as pay more than the cost of production, that is, than the ordinary rewards of the capital and labour concerned. The producers then make large profits. Now, see what happens. Anxious to secure these profits, the manufacturers produce more and more of the goods,—let us again say gloves; and perhaps other manufacturers begin a trade that is so profitable. At last they find they have made more than were wanted at the high price. They begin to be anxious to sell, and each offers them at a lower price than others, till the market price falls to the natural price. Thus, then, the price of manufactured goods is always less the greater the demand for them; and varies a little above, and a little below, the cost of production.

Goods which are absolutely limited in supply will rise in price to the highest amount which any buyer will give for them.

Goods, such as agricultural produce, are always dearer the greater the demand for them; and the price will be such as to pay the cost of production under the least favourable circumstances in which they are produced.

Goods, such as manufactured goods, are cheaper the greater the demand for them; and the price is always near the cost of production.

XIV.—PROPERTY.

THE value of goods does not consist in the labour bestowed upon them, but only upon the supply of, and the demand for, them. We do not pay a fisherman for his fish because he has toiled to catch them, but because his selling them to us saves us, when we want them, from the toil of catching them ourselves. If a man find a diamond by chance, he gets as much for it as another man does for one of the same size and quality which has cost him years of search. The purchaser pays the first man for saving him from such a number of years of search as the second has had; for no man who wishes to possess a diamond can calculate that he will be so lucky as to find one. The salmon that jumps into a fisherman's boat brings as high a price as the one that has required a whole night's fishing. The fisherman gets the price because he can supply our want,—whether by means of his labour or not we do not ask.

None of the labour by which nature produces goods for us is paid. Look at the labour involved in the glass of water we drink from a spring. It formed once a part of the salt waters of the great sea. The sun warmed it, sifted it from the salt, and lifted it up as vapour. The wind blew it on to the land. The cold upon the mountain tops of Britain condensed and froze it. Gravitation brought it down on to the hills as snow. The heat of the sun thawed it. Gravitation, ever at work, made it trickle down the mountain sides. Beds of gravel sucked it in and filtered it; and fluid pressure brings it up here to us, cool and refreshing. What a labour! and where is its value? It has none. Labour, as such, whether man's or nature's, has none.

But a water-carrier, who carries the water from the spring to the neighbouring town, gets a price for it there —or rather he gets a price for the service he has rendered to the inhabitants, and for the trouble he has saved them, in carrying it there. Now, notice, it costs him nothing at the spring, and might have been taken by any one else as well as by him. But since he has taken the trouble to collect it, and to bring it into the town, it is his; and whether he drinks it or sells it, we feel he has done nothing wrong. What a man bestows labour upon he expects the right to enjoy, or the right, if he chooses, to give the enjoyment of it to another, without let or hindrance; and our judgment approves of his having such a right. Property, then, is not robbery, as some men say; it is the right which a man has to make use of the results of his labour, or of not giving away these results except for something that will be equally satisfactory to him.

So, too, if I find a piece of iron, and seek a piece of wood that belongs to no one, and make a hammer, the hammer is clearly mine. The weight which nature has given to the hammer makes some one desire it, and I sell it for sixpence. The sixpence is now clearly mine, and the hammer is his who bought it. We can now answer two questions—" What is the foundation of property?" and " What is the extent of one's property in anything?" The foundation of property is the being the first to take anything to one's self, or to appropriate it, and the bestowal of useful labour upon it. The extent of a man's property in any kind of goods is the value of the useful labour which has been put upon it by himself, or by those who gave it him or sold it him, as that is estimated by those who purchase it.

That feeling, which is common to all men, of the **rights of property** which a man has in all that belongs to no one else, and upon which he has bestowed useful labour, is so strong that the laws and customs of nearly all nations have sought to protect property. There are some who say that law and custom is the only foundation of the rights of property. But that is not quite right. What a man has only by law would be no secure possession, for laws change. But it is acknowledged on all hands, at least in Great Britain, that if the law takes away a man's property the law does wrong. What the law cannot rightly take away it cannot give. It is because we feel it to be just that property exists. A thing which a man has taken from no one else, and has put labour into, that cannot henceforth be separated from it, is his by right and by justice; and these are above all law.

So much of the property that now exists has been taken in the old historical times from its former owners by conquest, or armed robbery, that some men can hardly believe there is such a thing as a rightful holding of property; and they are content to submit to a thing which they believe to be sanctioned more by law than by justice, because it has always been found that it is useful to society to protect property, and hurtful to take it away. If property be unsafe in the hands of its owners then no capital can be saved, because no one will labour to produce anything, when he cannot be certain that he himself will be allowed either to use or to save the fruits of his labours. In the days of King Stephen of England famine spread over the land. And why? Because everywhere were robber castles, and robber barons who wasted or trod down the corn-fields, and the farmer found that he might as well plough the sea as the land for all the corn he could get. He was not allowed to reap for himself, and therefore he ceased to plough and sow.

At the present time there are countries in which all that a man acquires is at the mercy of the rulers. Such countries, once fertile, have become deserts, for the want of cultivation. Where governments take all, poverty ensues. But some propose that the people of a country should take all that every man acquires from him, and that the whole thus taken should be equally divided among all the people. Private property, they say, should not be allowed to exist. This system of an equal distribution of goods is called **Communism,** sometimes it is called Socialism, sometimes Owenism, from the name of Robert Owen, who advocated the system in Great Britain. Let us suppose that these communists had their way, and see what would happen. All the property that men have saved must be taken and shared equally with all other men. Truly if this were done there would not be much for all. In England, each person it is calculated would have about thirty pounds a-year; in France, only nine pounds. But how is it to be done? The large houses and large factories, could they be divided? No! but they might be sold. But who is to buy them, since no one would have any private property? Again, when done, the skilful and industrious workman is not to be allowed to make anything for himself out of his skill and industry—the results of his labours are to be shared equally with the stupid and idle. He, then, will simply let his skill and industry lie waste. Why should he toil for those who will not or cannot toil for themselves? No one has capital; no one will work fairly, since he cannot get his fair reward; and nothing will be produced. Thus want and misery must ensue where the people, by law, forbid men to save and heap up for themselves, as surely as it has already ensued where government takes all to itself.

Two other systems similar to communism have been proposed, in which possession in common of the goods produced by all is to be maintained; but an attempt is made to allow the saving of capital. They are called, from the names of their proposers, St. Simonism and Fourierism. St. Simon proposed to allot to each man the kind of work for which he is best fitted, and to give to each a certain small share of his earnings as private property, the rest to be divided among all the people. But he did not show how those who allotted his work to each man were to be able to judge of what he could do best; nor yet how people with wills and minds of their own were to be brought to submit to such allotments.

Fourier proposed to divide the people of a country into groups of about two thousand, who were to live in detached localities of about a square league, under rulers of their own choice; and all, whether they could work or not, were to receive a certain lowest share of the produce of those who did work. The land was to belong to no individuals, but to the whole nation; and the produce left, after the lowest shares were dealt out, was to be given to each man or woman according to the rank which was allowed them by the votes of the others. Thus the idle were always to have the means of life, and the active and clever were only to get what might be allowed them by the rest. It is easy to see that the idle, under such a system, would never work, and the industrious would not do all they could; for what faith could they have that the votes of idle and envious men would give them their fair share?

But let us not be unjust to such systems. They were proposed by earnest men, who sought to do away with the evils that exist under the present system of private property, and the difficulties that hinder the working together of capital and labour; and who would fain have seen some change in what we see now—a few men excessively rich with little apparent labour, and a large number of honest, hard-working men who, strive as they may, remain poor—a number which seems to be constantly increasing.

The foundation of property is first occupation or possession of anything, and bestowal of useful labour upon it; not, as is sometimes said, the sanction of law and custom.
Communists say falsely that property is robbery. An equal distribution of goods would lead to general poverty.

XV.—RENT.

LET us suppose that a man goes out and occupies land in the wilds of America, where no one else is at the time an occupier. He fells the trees, drains the soil, and begins to raise crops. Now what will he get for it should he try to sell it? Only the price of the services he has put into it. For, if he were to ask more, the intending buyer would say, "No; I will clear land for myself rather than pay you more than the price of your labour and capital." Or if he try to sell the corn he has raised he will get no more than the cost of production of that corn. If he ask more, people will prefer to occupy new lands for themselves. For, as we have often seen, no one pays for the usefulness of the corn, or for the properties of the soil which makes the corn grow. Men pay only for the services of the proprietor, or rather for the trouble which he saves them of raising corn for themselves. And so long as there is plenty of unoccupied land in America or elsewhere, those who thus take it are allowed by most men to be the rightful owners.

But there comes a time when all the land of a country is thus occupied. This is the case in Great Britain, and in all Europe now. There is no more unoccupied land which any one can clear; and what is more, the proprietors of the land receive from the products of it, in most cases, far more than the ordinary payments for labour and the profits of capital. Usually, too, as if to make the thing worse, those who are proprietors now do not themselves live on the land, or work upon it. They let it to farmers, who put capital and labour into it, and are content to receive from the sale of the corn and other produce a share such as pays them its cost of production. All the rest of the price, often a large sum, is given to the landowner as rent; or, in towns, the owners of the land build houses for warehouses, factories, and the like, and let them to merchants or manufacturers. These carry on business in them, for which they are content to receive the ordinary profits of capital, and pay all the rest of the money which their business yields to the landlord as rent.

Rent, then, is the excess of the produce of any portion of land above the cost of production. It goes always to the landowner, whether he be himself the occupier of the land or not. If the usual produce of a farm bring £1,200 in the market, and the cost of production be only £900; then, in this country, the landlord will receive a rent of £300 a-year. And yet more, if by some invention, the twelve hundred pounds' worth of grain could be produced for half the present cost, namely £450, then the rent would be certain to rise to £750. If, at the same time, an increase of population should increase the demand for corn, so that the value of the twelve hundred pounds' worth rose to £1,600, nothing in this country would prevent the landowner from getting a rent of £1,150. This is what there is in landed property that makes it seem to be different from other kinds, namely, that after the first occupation and services, and when all the land in a country is occupied, the owner of any portion may receive an enormous increase of his share of the produce, without doing anything himself to increase it. There are lands in London which used to yield only £40 a-year of rent, and now yield £80,000, not from any new labour or capital applied to them, but merely because of the increase of people around them, and of the fact that occupiers are now willing to pay so much for the use of them.

This happens, not because land is anything different in its nature from other goods, but because it belongs to the first of the three classes of goods mentioned in the section on price, that, namely, of which the quantity cannot be increased by any means. It has, therefore, a monopoly price. Those who are willing to pay so much in London, might have unoccupied land in America for a dollar an acre, this payment being for the service of the American Government in making roads to it. But rather than take the trouble of clearing such land, they give the rents required in London. And, it is doubtful if the trouble of clearing it would be greater than that which the first clearers of land in Great Britain had. For what does unoccupied land mean? It is land covered with pestilential marshes—land infested with snakes, gliding among thorns and briars—land where fever wastes and kills the lonely pioneer; so that, however small may be the services of landowners in London now, those who first cleared their lands did render service. That which it is most important for us to remember now is, that these and all other services of labour or capital which have been put into the land since its first clearance, have been rendered in a form the supply of which cannot be increased, while the demand for it is ever increasing.

Thus property in land, though it presents itself to us in a form so startling, that of possessing what yields an ever increasing reward for services long since rendered, is certainly not unjust in its origin, any more than property in moveable goods—a barrel of water, or a sixpenny hammer. It depends upon the three facts

—first occupation, bestowal of labour, and possession by law.

"But," men say, "though perhaps not unjust in its origin, the progress of property has been the cause of injustice. The powers of the land, like those of the air, the water, and the electric fluid, are the gift of nature to all men. You, the landowners, have taken all those of land to yourselves. You keep us, who have no land, out of it. Happily for us, you could not appropriate the air, the waters, and the electric fluid. The law has sanctioned your possession so far; but, what the law does, it can undo. We admit the right you have to the ordinary profits of capital and wages of labour, but the rest should belong to the nation." Even in Great Britain, as well as abroad, such are the ideas spreading with regard to rents; and proposals have been made that all unearned increase of the rents of any land should henceforth belong to the nation; that is, to the Government. The danger of such proposals is, that they threaten the right to any kind of property, and, as we have seen, where that is insecure capital disappears, labour ceases, and misery reigns.

One thing ought to be noticed, that whether the rent be paid to the landowner or the Government, or whether the farmers were allowed to keep it, rent is a payment which cannot be escaped by those who use corn or any other farm produce, or who use lands for dwelling-places or warehouses. For some farms are more productive than others, some houses and shops are more desirable than others. These may remain as productive or as desirable, and yet worse lands will be cultivated, and less desirable sites built upon, because the produce or convenience which they yield is required. The extra produce of the better lands must belong to some one. If all the land were declared rent-free to-morrow, people would still have to pay the price which rewards the tillers of poor land, and the price of the extra quantity got from rich land would only go to the farmer, instead of to the landlord. From this, it is easy to see, too, that high rents do not raise the price of corn, for the price of corn is always that of the cost of production in the worst cultivated land, and rent is what remains over and above the cost of production in good land.

A famous writer, named Ricardo, states that rent is "payment made for the natural powers of the soil;" but, as we have shown, no payment is ever made for the natural powers of anything. The theory of rent, or explanation of its nature and origin, which this writer gives is very famous. He thinks that in any country the lands which are first tilled are those that yield food enough for the people with the least labour. By and by the people become more numerous. Then more grain is wanted; it becomes dearer; and farmers begin to till land that is not quite so fertile as the first. As time goes on, and the people increase, fields that are ever less fertile are taken in, because ever more is paid for corn. The last fields taken in are such that corn at its market price will just pay the cost of production; but the first fields, being fertile, yield corn at a much smaller cost of production. The difference between the cost of production in the poorest and the richer fields is the rent of the richer ones. The last taken in pay none; they will be farthest from towns, and in the more barren spots of a country, and are called the **margin of cultivation**.

This famous theory, like many others, is not quite true to facts. Men do not always till the richest fields first in a new country; and it is not the case that the least fruitful fields which men cultivate pay no rent. All the land of Great Britain, whether it be cultivated or not, pays rent of some kind. Some land, in which nothing is produced, as a fine site for a country or a coast house, pays a very high rent. And, in fact, different countries have different modes of paying rent, as well as different ways of deciding how much should be paid. Custom, not cost of production, rules the amount. There is in the most of Italy a mode of dividing the produce between the owner and the farmer equally, which is called the **metayer system** of rents. In some districts the owner gets two-thirds of the produce; in some he provides the cattle, seed, ploughs, &c.; in some again these are provided by the farmer.

Rent is the excess of the produce of any portion of land above the cost of production. Rents in some lands increase without any new services having been rendered.
Landowners are possessors of a commodity which in Europe is always at a monopoly price.
Ricardo's theory of rent is, that it is the price of the natural powers of the soil. The worst lands cultivated form the margin of cultivation.
Though rents were taken from the landowners they would still have to be paid to some one; and the price of corn would not be less.

XVI.—EDUCATION OF WORKMEN.

THE more efficient capital and labour can be made, the more wealth is produced. Capital is made more efficient by its savings being turned into machinery. How can labour be made more efficient? By savings, too, of a kind. For there is a capital which the workman has stored up in him, as these other savings are in machines. That is his skill, acquired by the learning and practice of his trade; and not merely his skill in handicraft, but all the other mental and moral qualities which make him a better workman and raise his wages. Since wages rise according to the disagreeableness or danger of his trade, according to the perseverance needful to learn it, according to his trustworthiness, anything which leads him to be more self-denying and to endure better what is disagreeable—anything which tends to make him more persevering in difficulties, and more faithful under temptation, will be a source of better work and better wages for him. Suppose all workmen were less to be trusted,—more eye-servants than they are now,—then the expense of more watchers must be added to the cost of production of all our goods, the demand for them would become less, labour would be less wanted, and wages must fall.

One thing that more than any other tends to make good and efficient workmen is education. Employers of labour long thought otherwise; and one may yet find in society remnants of a race who were won't to say that "two men who can't read are worth three that can." But experience has taught something better now. An educated soldier is found to be worth three uneducated, and it has been calculated that if we could get an army of educated recruits, we should save, in Britain, a million and a quarter pounds yearly in the training of them for soldiers.

Why is it that, in a country so rich as this, so few workmen are well educated? Because, till very lately, children instead of being sent to school were sent to work, and grew up ignorant and dull. Their little fingers could do some things better than those of men. And when the law sought to save them from labour in their infancy, capitalists, in the name of free trade, cried out that our commerce would be ruined. Happily, after a long series of attempts by means of different laws, the British Government has at last been able not only to save them from too early labour, but also to provide for their education. For education tends to make men prudent, and better able to judge how, by delaying an enjoyment now, a greater enjoyment may be had afterwards; thus savings are likely to become greater than ever before. Education, too, tends to show the utility, if nothing more, of being honest and honourable; thus less watching of workmen will be required. It will tend, too, to lighten the evil which the bringing in of new machinery causes. Those who learn science, learn how nature works—the reasons of things; and when their work is set aside by a new invention, they will be quickly able to turn to the new form of work required, or to some other trade. The source of the suffering from inventions has been not the machinery, but the ignorance of workmen, and their inability to adapt themselves to things new.

Ordinary book-learning, and a knowledge of the easier parts of science, such as common schools give, is called **primary education**. But a workman requires also a higher kind of education to fit him for his trade. His eye must be taught to judge correctly of sizes and shapes of things; his hand to handle tools and sketch plans of the things he makes. This is called **technical education**, and should be given in technical schools. For want of such schools in Great Britain, it is said that ours are being beaten by foreign tradesmen in the production of things good and cheap. Men of science make discoveries; but our workmen cannot apply them to trade as the better taught workmen of Belgium and Prussia can. Technical schools are needed, which would train up a class of foremen, or leaders of workmen, who would be able to adopt any new discovery in science, and direct common workmen. Without them, some men declare that we shall soon lose the position which the coal and iron of Britain gives us,—that of being the first manufacturing nation of the world.

It is interesting to look back upon the way in which our workmen in former times received their technical education. All trades, during what is called the Middle Ages, were carried on under the management of societies called guilds. By a law passed in the reign of Queen Elizabeth, no youth could become "free of a trade,"— that is, had a right to earn wages in any trade,—till he had served some master seven years as an apprentice. No matter how clever he might be, and how much sooner he could turn out proper work, he must spend his seven years in learning, too often under a tyrant. At the end of the seven years he became a "companion,"—a journeyman, as we should now call him; but, even yet, he must work in no other way than according to rules given him by the body of masters. As each town had its own guilds, he could only work in the district where he had learned. A shoemaker in London could not make shoes for the people of York; a glover of Newcastle was unfit to cover the hands of the people of Bristol; and, if he went and sought work there, the magistrates would put him on the tread-mill. Crushed under petty rules and hindrances like these, only a few ever pushed themselves forward to be masters. The rest of the journeymen passed their lives in indifference and dependence,—paying themselves for their forced submission to the masters by ill-using the apprentices. No one scarcely thought of inventing a machine to do work better and cheaper; or, if he did, his life became a torment, and all of the trade looked upon him as one who sought to ruin them.

Well, in the days of George the Third, Queen Elizabeth's law was altered, and no one (except certain lawyers) required to be an apprentice, in order to be free to work at what he pleased. Every one might henceforth work where he pleased. One would have thought that all workmen would have hailed such a change. But no; what the law now ceased to enforce, they began, in many cases, to enforce by customs among themselves. And still, the societies, which guide the business of most of the trades, insist that no master shall have above a certain number of apprentices for each journeyman. Hatters allow no more than two apprentices to ten journeymen. Shipwrights and printers will allow no one to work at their trade unless he have served an apprenticeship of seven years; and masons, unless he have served five years. The different trades try to compel obedience to these rules by means of their societies, called **trades unions.** When an employer refuses to obey them, the men employed by him leave their work till he does. This is called a **strike.** When a workman refuses to obey them, the other workmen of the trades union try to force obedience by means of annoyances, persecutions of different kinds, sometimes personal injury.

This one thing seems clear enough, that long apprenticeships do not require to be forced by workmen upon the youths of their own class. It is true that a man must learn to work before he can do it. But surely that will be secured by his finding that no one will employ him, if he cannot do what he professes to do. Such long apprenticeships are a robbery of a part of the life of a young man. In three years, at most, one could learn to be a printer; and in fewer, to be either a mason or a hatter. And, then, in most workshops, the teaching of apprentices is a sham. The apprentice has to teach himself, and all the good he gets is by looking on at others working. He has to find out for himself how to do what he is told. Besides, some of the best workmen have been those who were never bred to a trade. Lee, a Cambridge student, invented the stocking-frame; Cartwright, a poet, invented the power-loom; and Arkwright, a barber, by his inventions, made the cotton trade the greatest in Britain.

And then, that any body of workmen should seek to limit the number of their apprentices is a piece of gross cruelty to those who are to be the workmen of the next generation. Suppose that all trades were to do the same, and that, in all, the number of apprentices they will allow is a million, while there are a million and a half of sons of working men ready to learn a trade. Half a million are thus condemned by their own class to idleness and a waste of the best time of life. Workmen have much to suffer from many causes; but not the least of their evils are those which they inflict on one another. And such a system of apprenticeships not only prevents a skilful and clever young man from selling his labour when and where he best can, it even serves the purposes of employers better than it serves that of labourers. The employer gets journeyman work at apprentice wages by means of it. Among the many advantages which our commerce would derive from good technical schools, not the least would be that of rendering the apprenticeship system useless.

A workman's acquired skill in his trade is so much capital. Education tends to make labour more efficient.

After the education of primary schools, that of technical schools is needed to make proper workmen.

The old system of apprenticeship was a waste of young men's lives, and it is tyrannous to enforce it now.

XVII.—COMPETITION.

WHEN two or more strive after the same advantage it is called **competition.** Two masters, each trying to get the same workman into his service—two workmen trying to obtain the same appointment—two shopkeepers, each striving to sell more goods than the other—all these are competitors. The more employers that compete for one workman the higher wage the one that gets him must pay; the more workmen that want one place the less wage the one that gets it must demand; the more shopkeepers that are anxious to sell the same kind of goods the less will be the price of them. Now, employers, workmen, and shopkeepers are all producers of goods or services, which they desire to sell,—they form what we may call the class of producers—while the people who buy the goods or services for use form the class of consumers; and the greater the number of producers of goods who compete with each other in their desire to sell, the better it will be for the consumers, who must thereby obtain these goods all the cheaper; all the less above the cost of production in a regular market.

What is better for the consumers is of course not so agreeable to the producers. But all are consumers, while the producers of any kind of goods are only few in number. For every man is a consumer except in regard to the thing which he produces. A hatter is a consumer in all things except hats; and the cheaper everything except hats becomes the better for him. Thus, when all things are cheap the whole of the people get the benefit in all the things they use; and the few of each trade are put to the disadvantage of not getting as much money as they would like to get for the peculiar goods which they produce. They will still, however, get the cost of production; for, as we have seen, those who do not get that cease to produce goods.

Cheapness benefits everybody, and that which secures cheapness is competition. For the man who makes things for a small cost of production does not necessarily sell these things for a small sum of money. He wants the largest sum he can possibly get for them, and will only be content to take less, and something nearer the cost of production, when he sees that others do the same. Producers of course dislike competition; but a wise people, knowing its advantage in trade—and wise laws, which should always be made for the advantage of the whole people, not of one class—will rather favour it. Suppose that in a town only one man had the right to sell cloth. He would charge whatever price for it he pleased, would take no pains to produce good cloth, and would probably be disobliging and unkind besides; for no one could go elsewhere to buy cloth. Suppose, again, that in the whole country only a hundred families had the right to sell it, the result would be nearly the same; for though there would be some temptation for one of the hundred to sell cloth a little cheaper than the others, and get all the custom, there would be a greater for all of them to agree that none will undersell the others, and all will share the profits. Such rights as we have now supposed are called **monopolies.** Queen Elizabeth used to give her favourites such rights. The famous Earl of Essex had the sole right of selling sweet wines; and cloth, iron, tin, oil, glass, leather, vinegar, fruit, fish, were all given to some one favourite to sell. As the list was read in Parliament a member, provoked, asked, " Is bread not among the number?" and when told that it was not, said, "It soon shall be." The East Indian Company had at one time the monopoly of tea; and the Corn Laws, as they are called, which hindered foreigners from bringing corn into the country, gave to the farmers of Great Britain a monopoly of the sale of corn. Bread, by these laws, was brought into the number of monopolies.

In old times, the guilds in the different towns had a monopoly of the right to make and sell the goods which they made in their own localities; thus, as we have seen, a shoemaker of York could not make or sell shoes to the people of Lancaster. In all these cases, the whole of the people of the land were made to pay more for the goods than would have been the price had any one, whether foreign or native, been free to compete with the monopolist. Individuals received a benefit, but the public was robbed. On reading the history of our country one can hardly help wondering how it came that monopolies were not put an end to sooner. Free trade, that is, an equal right to every one, to foreigners as well as natives, to make and sell what he pleases, has only been the rule in Great Britain since the year 1854, when the Corn Laws were abolished. Such things as are now dear, are so because their cost of production is great. How much dearer they would have been, had the Corn Laws not been abolished, it would be hard to tell.

Workmen compete with workmen, and thus wages are kept low; but then the public get the benefit in the cheapness of all the goods produced by workmen, and, each workman gets the benefit in the cheap price of everything but that at which he works. So capitalist competes with capitalist, and each reduces the profits of the other, but the whole public are benefited, as well as each capitalist in all things but his own produce. In the same way nation competes with nation. Suppose that Great Britain alone had all the iron and coal in the world, then it is evident that the British people could charge all the rest of the world what price they pleased for these, and for such things as are manufactured by means of iron and coal. But Belgium and Germany compete with Great Britain, and in order that the rest of the world may buy Belgian and German goods, they try to make them better and cheaper than the British do. The British are thus compelled to exert themselves; and the result is that Great Britain and Belgium and Germany are compelled to work better, and to produce better goods, by their mutual competition, and the people of all the rest of the world have the advantage of it. But then, Germany, Belgium, and Great Britain get the advantage they lose in one way back in another. The people of Ceylon produce coffee, and spices, and cocoa nuts, and might, if they alone of all countries could do so, have charged the British people what they pleased for coffee, cocoa-nuts, and spices. But the people of Jamaica, and of nearly all tropical countries, compete with them, and thus the British get their coffee and other things all the cheaper. So, if France alone of all countries produced wine, the French could charge the people of all other countries a monopoly price; but Spain, the Rhine-land, Cape Colony, and other lands compete with them and hinder it. In the same way Russia, Prussia, and Canada, compete for the sale of corn to the world, and by this fact the corn is cheaper. On the whole, then, if we lose in iron and coal because of competition, we gain in everything which other countries produce; if the French lose in wines, they gain in iron and coal and all other things; if the people of Ceylon and Jamaica lose in coffee, they gain in all others also; and thus, if free trade and competition were allowed all over the world, each country would be, beyond a doubt, richer in having cheaply at its command all the goods produced by every other country.

Each gets its own produce easily, and has only to produce more than it needs itself of what it can produce easily in order to obtain commodities which it could not produce without great labour, or perhaps not at all by any amount of labour. By competition, the wines of Southern countries are carried cheaply to the children of the North; the wool of Australia clothes cheaply the shivering natives of Siberia; the cotton of America forms the cheap shirt of the British workman; the bark of South America comes to heal the fevers of the crowded towns of Europe; and the tea and coffee of the tropics cheer, at small expense, the long winter evenings of the colder zones. A brotherhood, as well as a rivalry, of nations is brought about, and men's selfishness and desire to establish their own country's commerce leads them to seek to undersell each other, and so to spread over all mankind the special gifts of nature to special regions.

Competition, however, like every other good thing, has its attendant evils. "It is the cause that one man grinds another," say its enemies, the communists. And that is true. But the only way of preventing that would be to grant monopolies—to let only one shopkeeper, or one company of shopkeepers, exist in every town and village, only one particular workman or set of workmen engage in any trade, and then submit to buy their goods or accept their labour at the price they choose to ask. And, indeed, we may have over-competition. Two gas companies, or two water companies in one town, with two sets of pipes, and sets of offices and works, where one might suffice, are sheer waste. So are two railways between neighbouring small towns. There can be only one reason for allowing them—the evil of a monopoly. In such a case, it is wiser, perhaps, to allow the monopoly. Let the law grant the field of operation to one company only, and demand that their work shall be of a certain quality, their prices never above a certain rate, and that when their profits exceed the average reward of abstinence, they shall cheapen their services. And this is what is usually done. Except in such cases, the mutual grinding of competition is better than the general extortion of monopoly.

By competition, the whole public receives the benefit of cheap production. Producers are few; consumers are all the nation, and, therefore, laws regarding commerce, should be in favour of consumers rather than producers.

Competition exists between nations as well as individuals, and spreads those benefits over the whole world which nature has bestowed only upon a few countries. Over-competition is an evil, but not so great an evil as monopoly.

XVIII.—TRADES UNIONS.

MANY men think more about their loss in one respect, as producers, than about their gain in all other respects as consumers; and hence we have numerous plans to diminish competition by those who dislike it. Employers of labour formerly got laws passed which fixed a low rate of wages. Such laws, as we learned before, were both useless and hurtful, and none such now exist. But workmen of the present time are earnest to have them fixed at a high and uniform rate for each trade. This they do not attempt by force of law, but by means of societies, formed for each trade, and called **Trades Unions**. For most trades branches, or lodges of the union, are set up in each district. The workmen in that district, who are members of the union, pay a certain sum weekly to the lodge. The business which concerns the whole of the trade is regulated in London, or some other large city, by a central committee of members from the different lodges who meet there. These unions serve other purposes as well as that of raising wages. They allow certain payments to men who are out of work, or sick, or for the funeral of a member; and the lodges convey to each other news of where work is to be had, and where wages are high. So far these societies are good, and by means of them workmen learn to save, and to work with, and for, their fellow-workmen.

Their chief objects, however, are to raise wages, and keep them at a high fixed rate the same for all workmen, and to shorten the hours of labour. This they do—

First, By insisting upon apprenticeships, and limiting the number of apprentices.

Second, By insisting that work should be done only in a certain way.

Third, By insisting that no man who is not a member

of the union should be engaged by an employer, and by cruel annoyances to workmen who are not members.

Fourth, By strikes.

Fifth, By agreements to work only nine hours a day.

We have already seen the evil and injustice done to young workmen by the system of apprenticeships. To insist that work should be done only in a certain way is a great evil to society, and a gross injustice to producers, who, knowing a better and cheaper way of doing work, are obliged to do it in a worse and dearer way. Either it deprives the labourers themselves of work, because foreign manufacturers who are not so hindered send goods rightly and cheaply made into our markets, and the demand for those made at home ceases, and with it the demand for workmen; or, if it happens, as in the building trade, that foreigners cannot supply the kind of goods, then this system of interference robs the public. The capitalist is obliged to make the goods as the union requires, but he will not do it without the usual profits on his capital. He is thus compelled to raise the prices of his goods, and the consumers have to pay dearly for goods not made in the best way. There is hardly any part of housebuilding which is not so made dear and bad; bricks are made, stones are cut, smith and carpenter work are done, all according to union rules. The employers get their profits, but society gets its houses slim and bad—so slim that sometimes, while being built, they fall upon the workmen themselves.

Most unions, though not all, refuse to allow piecework to be done; and require payment to be given for the time that a man works, not for the work he does. So that the longer a man can dawdle over work, the better he is paid; and the active workman gets only the same wage, though he may have done twice the work of another. This fixing of the same wage for all workmen, good and bad alike, is a sure way to make them all bad at last; it takes from the industrious man all motives to industry, and makes the lazy lazier still. For, why should they labour hard, when taking it easily does as well for them when pay-day comes? The employer is compelled to take so much from the wages of the good workmen to pay the bad ones; and then, when men become too old to do as much as the fixed wage requires, they are paid off.

The mode of forcing up wages, and of securing that an employer shall not engage men who are not members of the union, is by what is called a strike,—that is, a turn-out of all the workmen from the workshops in which the wage required is refused, or where the non-members are employed.

Of course, people have a perfect right to refuse to work for any one who pays them too little, or in whose works men are employed whom they do not choose to work beside. Every servant who engages with a master,—any one who engages to do any work,—must in a manner strike before the wage or price can be fixed. "I want eight pounds a term," says the servant. "I will give you seven," says the employer. "I will not take that," says the servant; "I will seek another master." "Very well, then, let it be eight pounds," says the master. "But, have you also hired Tom Black?" the servant asks. "No, but I intend to hire him," says the master. "Then I can't engage with you." "Why?" "Because he drinks and swears." "In that case I will not hire him," the master at last agrees; "for I prefer your services, even if I must lose his." And thus the bargain is struck; because the servant has practically struck for the two things required. The difference between such a bargain and a workman's strike is this. A man says to his employer, "If you do not give me thirty shillings a week, instead of twenty-eight, I will not work for you; and the five hundred other men in your works will also refuse to work for you, unless you give them the same. It is not my case only, but five hundred others you have to deal with." The power to say so comes from the workmen being combined in a trades union; and the power to make good what they say comes from the fact that the workmen who strike are supported by contributions from the other workmen of the whole union, who are not on strike.

Since, then, there is nothing wrong in a strike for raising wages, the thing that must be looked to is—whether it be prudent or not.

In the *first* place, strikes are seldom successful in raising wages. The workmen leave work; receive a sum of money from the funds of their unions; the money gets less weekly as the funds of the unions become smaller—is at last hardly enough to keep them alive; the master still refuses to grant the wage required; and, in the end, they are glad to go back to work for the old wage. This is the usual course of them. All the time has been lost; and the wages of the workmen, as well as the profits of the master, for the weeks during which the strike has lasted, have been thrown away. During a strike of the iron-workers of Staffordshire in 1865, three hundred and twenty thousand pounds in wages were lost; a fortnight's misery was caused to above two hundred thousand people; and, in the end, the workmen were beaten.

If, by any chance, an employer's profits were above the ordinary rate, then a strike of his workers might succeed. But what would be the result? The higher wages won would lead more workmen to enter the same employment, and the increased supply of labour would again bring down the wage. Of course, if by insisting upon apprenticeships, and by limiting the number of apprentices, they try to hinder this, the success, supposing it could be maintained, would be that of men who kept an advantage by force, by depriving other workmen of their right to labour as they please.

Where employers' profits are not above the usual rate, and a strike leads to a rise of wages, the only result that can come at last is, that the capital which is now receiving less than the ordinary reward must either be withdrawn from the trade altogether, or carried on elsewhere, where wages, and other circumstances, are such that the usual profits can be made. From this cause the silk trade of Spitalfields was removed to Paisley and Macclesfield; that of Coventry was broken up; the carpet trade of Kidderminster was removed to Kilmarnock; the shipbuilding trade of Newcastle went to Glasgow; and from this cause, too, that trade may soon have to remove from Glasgow.

In the *second* place, even if strikes are successful, they do not pay what they cost. The trades union is a heavy drain upon the pocket of the workman. There are weekly contributions to pay of ninepence, or a shilling, or more, entrance fees, quarterly payments, contingent funds, extraordinary levies, and fines, amounting to between three and four pounds at times. And much of the money thus drawn goes to pay secretaries and delegates their salaries and travelling expenses. It is true that some of the money is applied to the relief of the sick and of those out of work; but most of it goes to uphold strikes. In one year, lately, the mason's union of Scotland paid £5,383 for strikes, and only £1,550 for the other objects of the society. He that has ever seen a lot of workmen on strike, lounging at street corners, their backs against lamp posts, lean and hungry looking, and can guess what things are like in their homes where wives and children sit pining, may estimate, if he can, what a strike costs.

In the *third* place, a strike is always likelier to fail than to win. A workman with a wife and family cannot go without wages for months, whereas a man of capital has that to live upon, and may much more easily wait till workmen are able to endure no longer than they can till he is so. The workman has to want the means of life; the capitalist, if he makes any change, only cuts short his luxuries.

In the *fourth* place, it is commonly said that if a strike be successful, the men who win must rob some other labourers, for the wages fund having more taken from it in one trade, can pay less to some other. This is not wisely said. There is no such thing as a fixed fund, like that called the wages fund, and destined to be divided among labourers. But this is true, that wages depend

TRADES UNIONS.

upon the relation of the amount of capital in a trade to the number of tradesmen; and there is really no means of raising wages but by either increasing the capital or lessening the number of labourers. Now, as we have seen, a successful strike, if it diminish profits too much, tends rather to drive capital from the trade or the place; or, if it raise wages, it tends to bring new workmen to the trade and place, for the sake of the high wage.

In the *fifth* place, strikes can be matched by **lock-outs**. Masters combine into unions, as well as workmen, and make agreements about uniform fixed wages, which are quite as unfair as those of the workmen. The masters in the iron trade have a union in which the wages of the workmen are fixed every three months; and they enforce their decisions by means of lock-outs, as the workmen do theirs by means of strikes. Suppose the masters have agreed to lower wages, and the men have resolved to strike rather than submit. They intend to strike first in one work, and after the employer there is beaten, they will strike in another, then in another, and so on. The lock-out prevents this. When the men of one workshop strike, all the masters of the union close their works, so that the workmen of the district are all thrown out of work at the same time. A set of men in one work cannot then help another, and thus the masters cannot be taken one by one. A lock-out, then, is a strike of masters against workmen, and the end of such doings can only come when either will yield to the other, or some kind of half-way between what each wants is agreed upon—a compromise made.

Lastly, let it be noticed that strikes are not unjust; they are acts of the same kind as a merchant or manufacturer does when he holds on his goods and will not sell till prices rise. A strike is a holding on by the merchants who have labour to sell. When merchants refuse to sell, and hold out for higher prices, we admit that they know their business if they do not hold out too long, but sell at the right time before prices fall. So, strikes may prove that working men know their business, if not carried too far. The difficulty is, to know when the supply of labour and the capital ready to employ it are in such a state of balance that a change will drive capital away. It may be said that strikes are a means of finding out whether or not capital can afford to pay more for labour; but the workmen ought to remember that the competition of capitalists almost always keeps profits at the lowest point, and to strike in order to see whether it will be driven away or not, is like cutting open the bellows to see the wind.

Let us now consider how trades unions deal with workmen who will not become members, or who work at what they disapprove of, or at wages lower than they demand. Such a man's name they publish in black lists as a "knobstick" or a "black sheep," and order the lodges in the country to keep a sharp eye upon him whenever he travels to seek work. If he gets work anywhere, they steal his tools or maim his body. This is called "rattening," and is said to be the work of "Mary Ann," that being a pet name for the union. Not long since, the saw-grinders of Sheffield were guilty of crimes such as bring disgrace upon a country. Men met in a dark room, and were paid money by the agents of the union to blow up the house of a "knobstick" with gunpowder, and to shoot him at night in a lane. With shame it must be told that those who paid for, and those who did the dastardly work, are yet living in a sort of honour among the workmen of Sheffield. Let us hope that, as our fathers achieved their freedom from tyrannical governments in the olden time, the workmen of to-day will soon find means to rise up and successfully crush the tyranny of Mary Ann. Already, some have begun to attempt it.

Another of the objects of trades unions is to shorten hours of labour, without the pay being less. Nine hours a day they think long enough for a man to toil for daily bread; and, perhaps, they are right; perhaps, too, our bodily frame is so made that in nine hours' good work we can produce as efficiently as in ten, with the weariness which that brings on. But nothing is surely known as yet about the least number of hours in which men can do most work. And if ten hours' work, which is usual now, give one-tenth more produce than nine hours' work would do, then for men to ask nine of work with the pay for ten is simply to ask for a rise of wages. Whether employers can give it or not will depend entirely whether they had more than the ordinary profits before; and if not, and they be forced to grant the nine hours, then the prices of things must rise in order to yield these profits, and consumers, that is the public, will have to pay for the leisure won by the trades which get it; or, as is more likely, employers will seek out machines to do their work; or the trade may fall off, because of the increased price of the goods, the public dispensing with them as much as possible; or Belgium and France and Germany, which could not make them quite so cheaply as we before, may now find a place for their produce in our markets. And in any of these cases the nine hours' movement, though not wrong, will turn out what in this world of business is as serious as it is to be "wrong," namely, "foolish."

This subject of trades unions shows us an evil that threatens our trade. Capital and labour, neither of which can do without the other, are at implacable war, each weakening the other with mutual blows from strikes and lock-outs. Civil war rages, too, in the ranks of labour. Good workmen are being ground down to the level of bad ones, and the freedom of the working man is being taken away by a selfish organization of lodges. Some remedies for this state of things have been proposed, and it is certain that if no remedy can be found, capital will seek other countries; and labour here, as a consequence, will have neither tools to ratten nor wages to raise.

Trades unions are organizations which in some respects are good. In their main objects they seek to raise and equalize wages, and to reduce the hours of work. Their objects tend to drive capital from the country.

Strikes are seldom successful, and never, in the end, raise wages. Only one of two things can do that—increase the capital, or diminish the number of workmen. Lockouts are as unjustifiable as strikes. Shorter hours of labour being adopted may enable foreigners to beat us in our own markets.

XIX.—CO-OPERATION.

How shall the war between capital and labour be stopped? We, society, for whom they unitedly produce cheap commodities, are concerned that the strife should, as far as possible, cease. Some have proposed what are called **Boards of Arbitration,** made up of equal numbers of masters and workmen. The thing is done in Nottingham in the lace and hosiery trades, and seems, so far, to have worked well. But, at most, these boards only regulate the strife when it breaks out on some special point, they do not remove its cause. In fact, the tendency of arbitrators is always to divide the amount in dispute, not to remove the cause. Nor can the cause ever be wholly removed which brings labour and capital into conflict. It is true that, in a sense, their interests are the same, since the more capital there is the better for the labourers; and the more labour there is the better for the capitalists. But the interests of the buyers and sellers of labour can no more be wholly the same than the interests of any other buyers and sellers—the one wishes to receive much, the other to give little.

Co-operation, too, is a plan that has been proposed amid great shouting of philanthropists. By this is meant that workmen should be the owners of a part, however small, of the capital which their industry requires; and should, besides wages, receive a share of the profits of the business. It will thus be seen that only workmen who have saved something, or to whom charity or friendship will give something, can enter into a co-operative business. By means of co-operation capital and labour are united: the same man gets the reward both of abstinence and labour; his wages are changed into profits, in some cases it may be into losses. Co-operation, where it is found practicable, tends to make a very different being of the workman, from the gloomy hungry men who hang about the streets at the time of a strike. He becomes at once a responsible man; he works with energy; he does his own duty, and sees that others do theirs.

There are three different kinds of co-operative associations which have been formed with more or less success.

First, Those which produce or manufacture goods, the capital being lent by government, or formed by the savings of the members.

Second, Those which are merely stores to sell goods for the benefit of the members.

Third, Those which are formed for lending capital to the members, by which each may become a capitalist in his own trade.

After the Revolution of 1848, in France, the government sought to encourage co-operation of workmen, and voted £120,000 to lend them as capital. Fifty-six societies in Paris received loans; fourteen are all that now remain at work. Those which received most help from government were the least fortunate; but some, by dint of manly toil and endurance, have proved that co-operation can do something to improve the position of workmen. Fifteen printers, by a loan of £3,200, bought the trade and warehouse of the publisher Renouard. One-fourth of every man's wage was laid aside to repay the loan. They declared that their sole object was to save and possess property; and thus they separated themselves at once from the communists, who, there is reason to fear, were the chief borrowers in the societies that have failed. In ten years the debt was repaid, and a capital of £7,000 acquired. The society flourishes still; and let us notice this, its manager has all the power of directing the business.

The Co-operative Masons' Society of Paris was formed

without any help from Government; but part of their capital was, and is, lent them by people who are not masons, and they employ workmen who are not members; so far they are not strictly co-operative. They began in 1848 with £14, 10s. of capital; now they possess above £10,000. The pianoforte makers of Paris started the same year with £9 of their own, and nothing from government. They do all by piecework, which would not suit the most of our trades unions. Thus the skilful and industrious receive the reward of their industry. Ten months after their start they had a capital of £1,300. In all the associations the strictest watch is kept over the morals and conduct of the members; fines or expulsion follow the slightest breach of trust; in fact the successful associations began to reform society by first reforming themselves.

In the county of Suffolk, a gentleman named Gurdon has made two successful trials in farming by co-operation. In each case, an advance of £400, without interest, and of sixty or seventy acres to fifteen or sixteen farm labourers, has led the men so to work that their debts are cleared, their farms enlarged, and they can pay now a good rent for the land. No land, it is said, is better farmed, and no rents are paid more regularly.

But the co-operation of Great Britain takes, for the most part, the form of co-operative stores—to sell, not to produce. The most famous of these is that of the Rochdale Pioneers. It began in 1844, with a capital formed by the weekly contributions of a few poor men, sufficient to buy a chest of tea and a hogshead of sugar. No costly shop was kept to attract customers, and all sales were for ready money. The profits being all divided among the purchasers, shows that it is an association in which, not the capitalist and the labourer, but the capitalist and the consumer are combined. By careful management their business has extended beyond the sale of groceries; they have meat stores, drapery stores, a mill, a bakery, a reading room, a lecture room, and a cotton factory. So far, they have become producers. Their capital amounts now to about £50,000. There is a similar society for selling goods in Leeds; and, of societies for production of goods, there is one of pianomakers, one of gilders, and one of cabinetmakers in London; one of tailors, of hatters, of shoemakers, of cotton weavers, in Manchester; as well as others elsewhere.

In Germany, co-operation takes the form of societies of mutual credit. The savings of the poor are joined, and it is said that there are about nine hundred rich banks thus formed. These banks lend the money, but only to members, and for a term of three or six months. Any member can borrow, on his own promise to repay, as much as the amount of his share in the bank; but, if he wishes more, other members are required to become security for him. When a number borrow as partners for carrying on any trade, each of the borrowers is answerable for the whole debt with all his property. Thus, workmen lend to workmen, and all may become capitalists, and money is lent for the benefit of the borrower, not of the lender. But even here, the lender gets the reward of abstinence; for interest is received on the money borrowed, and as it is lent about three times each year, the profits of the bank are between eight and ten per cent.

All these examples show that co-operation is not a dream,—that it can do much to help workmen. But that it can do away with competition, as some think, is absurd, and certainly undesirable. For what could be put in the place of it but the monopoly of some huge association? And if this be not done, then associations must compete with each other, and society will reap the benefit. The watching of each other's conduct is one good point gained by it for workmen. In them every lazy member is a robber,—every dissipated one a disturber. But it must not be forgotten that all such watching is a deprivation of freedom; and the black lists of the trades unions show the abuse to which it tends.

Then the direction of the business forms a difficulty in co-operation. The business of an individual capitalist succeeds mainly because what he does he does for himself, and as he pleases; and he knows that fortune or failure for himself depends upon his acts. Now, though the interest of the workman in a co-operative workshop is great, it is that of a number. If they give one all the power, are they better than they would be under an individual capitalist, whom competition compels to pay them as highly as possible? If they seek to control him too much, then he may be powerless to act at some moment when a quick decision might have been a great gain, or saved a heavy loss.

Can co-operation prevent low wages? No; for different societies must compete, and thus lower wages as well as profits; or, otherwise, we must have monopoly in the form of an association of associations.

The good which co-operation seems to do is that of encouraging workmen to save, and making them earnest and faithful workers. The societies insist upon ready-money payments, and thus keep the poor members from running into debt. Since their members are also their customers in the store associations, they probably also supply them with genuine goods. In all these respects co-operation only does in a special way what all other inducements to save may do as well; and, in fact, its chief value is as a mode of education for the working classes. The evil which it seems most to threaten is loss of liberty to the individual workman, and the strengthening of the prejudices of their class by the power of union. Fortunately, one thing which it cannot put a stop to is competition.

By means of what are called **industrial partnerships**, working men are also led to become partly capitalists. For instance, the proprietors of a colliery in Yorkshire, in order to put an end to the strikes of their workmen, divided their business into a very large number of small shares, kept two-thirds of these and the management of the whole to themselves, and sold the remaining third to those of their workmen who had saved enough to buy them. The strikes have been averted, and the workmen work like men who know they are working for themselves. The same thing has been done by other firms both in England and France, with the same success; and thus industrial partnerships seem to present a mode, less widely talked of than co-operation, but equally hopeful, of reconciling labour with capital.

Co-operation tends to unite the capitalist and the labourer in one person. In England, co-operative stores are chiefly formed; in France, manufactories; in Germany, banks.

Co-operation tends to make workmen industrious and responsible; but it interferes with their freedom.

Industrial partnerships also tend to unite the capitalist and the labourer in one person.

XX.—TAXES.

To work well, or indeed to work at all, a man must be sure that he will reap the reward of his labour. He must either himself be able to watch that no one robs him, or, if others watch for him, they must be paid for the trouble they save to him. His own work being in that case so much the more productive, he can afford to pay them. A good government, with its array of soldiers, its ships of war, police, magistrates, and prisons, renders to its subjects this service, and receives taxes in return. Taxes, therefore, are the price of protection; and so needful is protection that it has been said even the worst government is better than none.

There is this difference between our purchase of other commodities and that of protection from government— we may buy the others or not, as we please, but that we must buy, or at least pay for. For other goods, too, we pay more or less according to the supply and demand; for protection we must pay such taxes as the government orders. No man can be allowed to say—"I will protect my own house and my own fields, and all those who are dear to me, by my own weapons, and will myself keep back both foreign foes and robbers at home." The measures which a government takes for the safety of a country protect all who are in that country; they cannot help receiving that protection, and cannot, therefore, be allowed to escape payment of taxes. Nor can he say—"I don't want the present government to protect me. I will rather pay taxes to King James than to King William." A government, to be really a protecting government, must have all the power needful to protect everybody, and can allow no competition with itself, for those who had wronged any one would seek shelter with the competing power, and thus, as happens in civil wars, many an act of plunder would escape unpunished. There is, therefore, no choice but for a nation to have only one government, with a right to demand what it pleases for the protection it gives, and for that nation to use its power as a whole people to make the government demand only what is reasonable.

It may seem at first sight that every one should pay taxes according to the amount of protection which he or she needs. In that way the poor, women, children, blind people, and the insane should pay most. It is easy on reflection to see, however, that not those who most need protection, but those who have most to protect, are rightly made to pay most; and, therefore, "men should pay taxes according to their riches." That is the first rule to which taxes should conform. A second is that "the amount which each has to pay should be always a certain and known sum." A third is that "a tax should always be taken by the tax-gatherer when it can, and as it can, most easily be paid." A fourth is that "no more than is needful for protection should be taken, and the sum needful for collection of taxes should always be the least possible;" and a fifth, that "the people who use luxuries should pay taxes out of them, while those who have nothing but the necessaries of life should be taxed as lightly as possible."

Taxes may be divided into national and local. A national tax is one which is paid by all the people of the land, and is ordered by Act of Parliament, the service for which it is rendered being given to the whole nation by the government. A local tax is one paid by the people of any district or town to its magistrates for special protection in that town or district alone.

The chief national taxes are, *First*, Those which are paid on houses, land, warehouses, mines, and other property, and called the **house, land,** and **property taxes.** *Second,* The **income tax,** which is a certain proportion of the incomes of all who have above £100 a-year. *Third,* Taxes on certain things kept and used by individuals, such as dogs, guns, horses, male servants. These are called **assessed taxes.** *Fourth,* Taxes paid for leave to carry on certain businesses, such as spirit dealing and hawking goods. These are called **licences.** *Fifth,* Taxes paid on receiving a legacy or falling heir to a property, called **legacy** and **succession duties.** *Sixth,* Those for stamps on business papers, such as receipts, and called **stamp taxes.** All taxes on goods may be called **duties**; those on goods brought from abroad are called **customs,** and are collected by custom-house officers; those on goods manufactured at home are called **excise duties,** or dues, and are collected by the officers of excise.

Local taxes are commonly called **rates.** Those which are paid for police, prisons, magistrates, paving, and lighting of towns are called **burgh rates;** in small towns, where there is no prison, the people pay a **police rate,** and for the prison used by the whole county, a **county rate;** for the repair of roads and streets a **highway rate** is paid; for the relief of the poor and support of the poorhouse, a **poor rate**; and for the education of children in national schools, a **school rate.**

Taxes may also be divided into direct and indirect. Direct taxes are money payments made to the tax-gatherer, and the man who pays them to him remains so much the poorer. Indirect taxes are really paid by those who buy goods that are taxed to consume them, and the man who first pays the money to government on account of the goods gets it back in the price of the goods when paid by the consumer. The falling of the payment of a tax upon the person who has to bear the loss of it at last is called the **incidence** of taxation. The incidence, then, of a direct tax is always upon the person who pays it to government; that of an indirect tax is upon the consumer. The income tax and all local taxes are direct; a tax on tea is an indirect tax, so is one on wine. If a tax be laid upon tea or wine, and the importer be made to pay it when he brings it into the country, then, when he sells them to a wholesale merchant, he must charge not only the price of the wine or tea, but also the tax, and the interest on the tax. The wholesale dealer, in selling it to the retailer, does the same, and the retailer does the same to the purchaser; and by the time he gets the tea or wine for consumption the amount paid to government may have been doubled. Therefore taxes on goods should always be made payable as nearly as possible to the time of consumption. Hence we may see the use of **bonding houses.** These are government stores, at the seaports, in which a foreign merchant may store his goods without paying duty. They lie there in bond, as it is called, till they are sold, and when they are taken away the duty is paid. A tax placed on raw materials increases like one paid by the importer of goods. If raw cotton were taxed to the importer, he would demand interest for the tax from the first purchaser, the first from the second, and so on. If the cotton have to pass through six different hands before it is made into a shirt and sold, then the purchaser has to pay the sum of the interest of all the six, far more than the government really gets by the tax.

The national taxes pay not only for the protection now received, but also the interest on debts into which former governments ran while carrying on wars to protect our forefathers from foreign enemies. It is in vain for us to say that these wars were useless, or wicked; the money was borrowed, and we who have inherited the capital heaped up by our forefathers—the roads, the harbours, the improvements in the fields, the stately public buildings in towns—not to speak of the freedom they achieved and the rights they secured, often by their blood—must take the bad with the good, and accept the consequences of their errors as well as of their industry and bravery. These debts are called the **National Debt**. It amounts to about eight hundred million pounds, and its yearly interest to about twenty-six millions. This absorbs more than half of what we pay in taxes. It has been calculated that of every pound now paid in taxes, twopence goes to the queen and royal family, eightpence to judges and other officers, a penny in pensions to old servants of the government, six shillings and sixpence in support of the army and navy, elevenpence to those who collect the taxes, and eleven shillings and eightpence for the interest of the national debt. Modern Governments usually pay the expenses of a war by the taxes raised during the time of the war, and thus avoid heaping debt on the head of posterity.

Some people have been so foolish as to say that a national debt is no evil, because those to whom the government pays the interest spend it in the country. But if I have paid this year six pounds in taxes, does the six times eleven and eightpence come back to me? A fundholder has received it, who may, indeed, have occasion to pay me as much as three pounds ten shillings, but that will be because I have given him goods or rendered him service for the money. The taxes I pay may well be spent in the country, but they leave me the poorer. I have first to earn the money to pay the tax, and then I have to do the work which brings me in what any government creditor happens to pay me.

There are people who wish that all taxes were direct, others favour indirect taxation. It is said that indirect taxes cost much to collect; they take more from the people than the government gets, and it is not easy to know when a government gets too much or too little out of them. Besides, direct taxes irritate people who forget that they are purchasing protection when they pay them, but indirect taxes prevent this feeling. As it is always painful to pay taxes, it is better to hide the doing of it under the form of purchasing something one likes, as tea, coffee, or wine. Direct taxation is like cutting off a piece of a patient's flesh without disguise, and giving all the pain; indirect taxation is like cutting it away while the patient is asleep under chloroform.

Taxes are payments for the services of government. They are not, like other services, subject to the law of supply and demand. A nation can but have one government.

Taxes are local and national, direct and indirect. The national debt was incurred by former governments in rendering services to our forefathers, and cannot honourably be repudiated.

XXI.—FREE TRADE.

CAN our government take taxes from the people of other countries to whom it renders no protection? Not directly; but it may tax the goods which our nation **exports**, or sends out to be sold to other nations. These foreign people would then have to pay dearer for the goods, to reward the exporter both for the cost of production and the tax. Such a tax would probably cause the foreign nation to buy the same goods from others, who can produce them cheaper, rather than from our merchants; or to give up the use of the goods altogether, and use something else instead. So we should lose our trade.

Our government, until very recently, used to tax the goods which foreigners imported or brought into our country—not, let it be noticed, to pay for services rendered to the foreigner, but to prevent him from competing in our markets. The tax made the goods he brought dearer than the same goods could be produced by some one at home. Foreign corn was, till 1845, taxed heavily by what are called **import duties**; and thus the government gave a monopoly of the sale of corn to the landowners and farmers of Great Britain. This system of taxing is called **protection**, and the people who admire it **protectionists**. In 1845 the Corn Laws were abolished, and the system of free trade, rather than that of protection, adopted in the making of laws about commerce. The commerce of Great Britain has increased wondrously since that time.

But some say there are foreign countries which do not allow British goods to be carried into them free from taxation; why should we not tax their goods? Those who say so call themselves **reciprocal free traders**, but they are really protectionists, favouring the monopoly of a few producers, and high prices paid by consumers. Though other countries may be foolish enough to make our goods dear to themselves, and to enrich, by a monopoly, the producers of like goods among their inhabitants, why should we make their goods dear to us by giving a monopoly to the producers of goods like theirs in Great Britain? Suppose the French can sell us silk at six shillings a yard, for which our manufacturers would charge eight, are we by a tax to raise French silk to eight shillings, and force ourselves to pay it, because they like to pay dear for our coal and iron? Let them do so if they will, but let us have the benefit of their cheapness in silks.

Those who wished, or who wish still, to prevent the competition of foreigners with our producers at home used to say that a nation ought to suffice for itself in what it produces. In time of war, if it depend on foreigners, that nation is liable to be deprived of the goods it has been accustomed to from abroad; and then, not being used to produce them itself, want must ensue. But if we depend upon foreigners for any commodity, it must be because they can produce it better and cheaper than we can. And if we get their goods, do they get nothing from us? They get our produce in return; and, in case of war, if we have to go without their commodity, they will also have to go without ours. It seems clear, then, that when a system of free trade is once established between two countries, each of which produces what the other wants, war can hardly arise between them, because each would thereby lose its accustomed benefit of cheap commodities.

For people in Great Britain to speak of being independent of foreign countries is, when one thinks of it, truly absurd. Look at our every-day comforts as well as at our principal luxuries. Almost every blade of wheat and corn that waves in autumn over the fields has been nourished by foreign guano; our cotton shirts come from America; our coffee from Mocha or Ceylon; our wines from France or Spain; our children are amused with foreign toys; our fine ladies shine in foreign pearls; our public halls are decorated with statues cut in foreign marble; our libraries are filled with books by authors of Greece, Rome, France, and Germany; our judges lay down the law clad in ermine from polar countries; in our schools we study arithmetic and algebra from Arabia, and geometry which came from Alexandria. Independent of foreigners! why should not the whole world contribute to our comfort, and the workmen of the whole world work for us? since, by what they take from us in return, they give employment to our workmen.

For this was another protectionist argument, that to bring in goods from abroad gave less work to our workmen who produce the same kind of goods. True; but if it took from them the home market for commodities which they could only produce with great labour and a heavy cost of production, it gave them in return the market of the most of the world for goods which they can produce easily and cheaply.

Sometimes, and for a number of reasons, certain commodities have been altogether prohibited from entering the country, or the taxes on them have been made so excessively high that it was evident the goods were meant to be kept out altogether. A worse result than dearness comes from such prohibitions. Men begin to smuggle these foreign goods; they are thus led into a life of habitual law-breaking; become desperate characters—robbers—and sometimes murderers, in their fights with coast-guards. Laws that are entirely prohibitive are useless as prohibitions, and cause a part of the population to grow up and to live heedless of all law.

There are two modes by which governments grant monopolies for a time to individuals—that is, by **patents** and **copyright**. A patent is the right which is given to the man who invents any useful machine, or who introduces any hitherto unknown art into the country, to be for seven—or it may be fourteen years, the only maker and user of that machine, or producer by means of that art. Although political economy condemns monopolies in general, yet no one can deny that he who gives to the world the benefits which new inventions bring should receive a high reward. Inventors have, for the most part, spent their lives in attempts which failed before they finally achieved success. They have sat late and early, spent health and wealth; and if there had been no hope of a special reward—if they had been aware that when they were at last successful, any other producer would be as free to use their machine as they themselves were—they would certainly not have persevered, and the machine would therefore not have been invented. If patents, then, were abolished, some other means must be found to encourage men of genius and skill to invent. In truth, it is not quite clear that patents are the best way of rewarding real inventors. Many of them are very poor. Money must be spent in courts of law in order to secure the monopoly; and hence an inventor has often to grant the main part of his reward to some capitalist, who is thereby induced to advance the money by which the patent is obtained. Nor is that all. A man may invent a machine, and find that some one who has had a hint of his plans has been before him, and obtained a patent; or, as often happens, two men have hit upon the machine at nearly the same time, and the mere accident of having been the first to apply for the patent gives the monopoly to one rather than the other.

If a man has a right to the results of his invention for seven or fourteen years, why has he not that right always? Because such fruits of invention cannot be considered the same as property. Other persons could have, and probably would have, soon invented the same machine; but two persons could never have built the same house, or enclosed and cultivated the same field.

Copyright is the right which the author of a book, or an artist who draws an original design, has to be the sole producer of copies of that book or design for a certain number of years—forty-two, at least. This monopoly is as justifiable as a patent; and might, perhaps, with justice be made more like the holding of property than patents are. For no two men could have ever produced the same book, so that there can be no doubt about the author, unless when concealment is intentional. And then, the public loses nothing by this monopoly; for the ideas and the knowledge to be got from the book may be taught and retaught in other words, and with new illustrations; it is only the words, or text, of the author, that all but he, or those to whom he sells the copyright, are forbidden to produce.

Taxes on exports tend to reduce our foreign trade. Taxes on imports were imposed to protect producers at home, and made home produce dearer to consumers. Reciprocal free trade is another form of protection. Many of our daily comforts and modern luxuries are of foreign production.

Patents and copyrights are monopolies, justifiable as rewards to inventors and authors, and are not rights like those of property, but only vrivileges granted for a time.

XXII.—CREDIT AND BANKS.

So far, we have thought and spoken of capitalists who provide materials, tools, and wages for workmen, as if they always did so only with their own savings. But one man may employ labour with the savings of another, that is, he may have **credit**; for **credit** is the power to use other men's goods. The power, it is true, may be given directly by the real owner to the man who uses it, as a loan; but usually bankers are the agents, by means of whom the capital of one is lent to another that he may use it in production.

A widow, for example, who knows nothing about business, has a little money left her, which she does not at present want. What will she do with it? To spend it would be foolish; to lay it past in a drawer might be a temptation to robbers. She takes it to the bank, and places it in the hands of the banker. This she does, because she knows the bank is well fitted for the safe keeping of money, and that the banker is wealthy and able to give it back to her at any time; and, because, for every hundred pounds there are of it, he will give her between two and three pounds of yearly interest. The farmer who has a little money by him which he does not need for his farm at present, does the same as the widow, for the same reasons, and so do all others who have money by them—too little to make a business by itself, and too much to keep useless. There is no such thing as hoarding or locking past money in secret places now, as there was in old times, except among the very ignorant. Now, what does the banker do with all these sums? He lends them to producers of goods whom he thinks trustworthy, sells, that is, the use of these savings, by charging from these producers five or more per cent. Thus he can easily afford to give those who entrust him with it between two and three per cent. The difference is his profit.

In this way, banks make use of savings. All petty sums like these unite as small streams into a river, and form, in the hands of those who borrow them, so much productive capital. We see then how a banker is an agent for turning inactive wealth into capital.

It must be evident now that credit is not capital, though the contrary is often asserted. Credit is the power to use other peoples' savings. It is the means of making what would otherwise be idle savings into capital, and the man who has credit can gain more wealth than he could do without it.

Banks prevent waste of wealth. The people who deal with banks may deposit daily the money they receive and do not want at once, receiving interest on it, and they can always draw out what they require. Thus, no savings need lie idle at any time. But it is chiefly by the use of **bank notes** that they prevent a waste of wealth. The banker is himself known, and believed to be a wealthy man, always able to repay to others what they deposit in his hands. He has credit with the public; and, therefore, his promise to pay is as good as actual payment. That being the case, those who come to him for the use of the savings deposited with him, or of his own money, take from him willingly not actual gold or silver, but his promise to pay gold and silver whenever it is required.

Now, see how this arrangement economises wealth. In the first place, the actual gold and silver is not sent out to be worn by passing from hand to hand; and the banker is enabled to make his wealth go much farther than he otherwise could. For he finds that, in order to keep all his promises, it is not needful to have beside him as much gold or silver as he has promised. One-third of the amount promised in notes serves for those who occasionally need money in gold or silver. If, then, between his own wealth and that of those who deposit with him he have, say, a million of pounds in gold and silver; he can lend a million in notes, and two-thirds of a million in coin, keeping beside him the one-third of a million for those who wish coin. Thus savings of one million have actually been turned into capital of one million and two-thirds of a million, and the banker makes a large profit; for, by deposits of one million at about $2\frac{1}{2}$ per cent. he gains interest on $1\frac{2}{3}$ millions at five, perhaps more, per cent.

Banks enable business to be carried on, without much carriage of money from place to place, by means of **bills of exchange** and **cheques.** Harry in London owes Jacques in Paris a thousand pounds for wine; and Louis in Paris owes John in London a thousand pounds for English goods. Harry should send Jacques a thousand, and Louis should send John a thousand. But if, instead, Harry give John a thousand pounds, and Louis give Jacques a thousand, then each has got his own, and no gold has crossed the channel. All this would be done by Louis finding out Jacques, giving him the money, and getting a letter from him to Harry, requesting Harry to pay a thousand pounds to John. Such a letter is called a bill of exchange, and Louis is said to buy the bill from Jacques. And it is evident that any number of groups of four, two and two, in any two distant places could always settle their accounts so, if they knew each other, and the sums owing from and to each town were equal. This would require, however, that the debtors should be always able to find the creditors in each town, and buy bills of exchange from them. Banks furnish the means of doing this handily, for they buy bills from creditors and sell them again to the debtors.

If the amount owing by all the debtors in one country, say France, for the goods they have received from the other country, say England, be exactly equal to the amount owing by debtors in England to creditors in France, then no money requires to be sent from the one country to the other, and the rate of exchange between the two countries is said to be at par. But if Frenchmen owe more to Englishmen than Englishmen to Frenchmen, then, it is evident, that after all the bills have been exchanged by means of the banks, some coin would still require to be sent from France to England. The French debtors will seek to avoid this trouble and risk by offering to pay a little more than the sums they owe for bills —perhaps ten shillings a hundred pounds. Bills in France are then said to be at a **premium**. In England, on the contrary, bills payable in France will be easily got, and on that account English debtors will need to pay a little less than the sums they owe. Bills in England are said then to be at a **discount**. The **rate of exchange**, or the **balance of trade** is said to be then in favour of England and against France; and this really means that more goods have been sold by England to France than by France to England. There will be times, of course, when the balance of trade is in favour of France and against England.

It was once thought to be a sign of prosperity in a country when it had more money to receive from other countries than it had to pay to them. Laws were made with the aim, as much as possible, to keep the imports less than the exports, for the difference should always come in as money. This was done under the false idea that money is wealth; and the system of trading under which such laws were passed is called commonly the **mercantile system**.

The carriage of money from one country to another is also saved by banks giving what are called **circular notes**. A person with money in a bank wishes to go abroad. He does not take gold from his banker, but gets a letter of credit from him to other bankers in Paris, Frankfort, anywhere, asking them to pay him a certain amount. His banker and these others have business together; and in the case in which the balance of trade is in favour of England, these bankers, when they give the traveller his money, help to pay the debts of their country to England without transmitting coin.

The man who grants a bill of exchange is said to draw upon his debtor. Persons in the same town can also draw upon each other in a similar way. Buyers of goods often get credit for three or six months from the sellers. Now the sellers are often in want of money for immediate use. They draw upon the buyer, by writing him a short letter, requesting him to pay the money to their order at the time when it is due. The buyer agrees to this by writing his name on the letter, which is called a **draft**, or **bill**, and is then said to accept the bill. The seller then takes the bill to a banker, who pays him the money, taking off discount. Before it is paid, however, the seller writes his name on the back of the bill. This is called **endorsing** it, and means that if the buyer fails to pay the money at the time when it is due, he, the seller, will pay it himself.

Sometimes those who draw a bill, instead of taking it to the banker to be discounted, pay it away as they would pay a bank note, having first endorsed it. Those who get it may endorse it also, and pay it again; and thus it may change hands many a time before the day when the acceptor should pay the money. If the acceptor fails to pay, all who have endorsed it, in the order of their signatures, are liable to be called on to pay, if all those who endorsed it before them have also failed.

Sometimes one man draws upon another, who accepts, when no goods have actually been sold by the one to the other. Such drafts are called **accommodation bills**. As there is no real buying and selling in the case, prudent tradesmen and bankers will have nothing to do with them.

A man who has money in a banker's hands, instead of paying his accounts by coin or notes, sometimes pays by means of a written order on his banker. Such an order is called a **cheque**. It is really a bill drawn by a depositor upon his banker, and saves the use of money. All bills of exchange, and cheques, and drafts are taxed, and must be written on stamped paper; the stamp shows that the tax has been paid.

These bills of exchange and cheques of different kinds, which may pass from hand to hand like money, till the actual money they are drawn for becomes payable by the acceptor, are all cleared, often without any actual payment of money, by an exchange between the different banks to which they are sent. For the English banks, this takes place at the clearing house in London. Clerks attend there from the different banks with all the cheques that have been paid into each bank during the day. About ten thousand million pounds in cheques are exchanged here in a year, and as the differences of the amounts of the cheques or bills need only to be paid, a very small sum of money may suffice.

Banks convert petty savings, which would otherwise be unproductive of interest, into capital. They prevent waste of wealth. Bank notes, bills of exchange, and cheques, are representatives of wealth—promises or orders to pay made by the owners of wealth.

By bills of exchange the transmission of money from one country to another is rendered unnecessary. At the Clearing House, by an exchange of bills between different banks, large accounts are settled without actual payment of money.

XXIII.—PAPER MONEY AND SAVINGS BANKS.

BANK notes, bills of exchange, and cheques are used as money and instead of it; they are so many representatives of wealth, in addition to the actual money of gold and silver. Now, if gold and silver coins be plentiful, the prices of all other things are high; and if they become less in supply, the prices of other things fall. In the shape of notes, bills, and cheques, we have enormous additions made to these representatives of wealth. Their effect is the same as if the number of coins had been increased to the same extent—they raise the prices of all other commodities.

Paper money, whether notes or bills, makes commodities dearer in another way, as well as by increasing the quantity of money. It is given by bankers as credit, and by means of it merchants are able to buy more goods than they would otherwise have done. The demand for goods is thus increased, and their prices therefore rise. Bank notes cause increase of prices in this way more than bills or cheques: for these only represent money from their date till they become payable, while notes remain long in circulation.

Since the year 1850, large quantities of gold have been brought to this country from California and Australia. The supply of that metal has been three times greater during that period than it was before. This gold, if it had all been coined into money, would have greatly raised the prices of commodities, since it would have lowered the value of gold in relation to them—its supply being increased and theirs remaining the same. But, fortunately, at the same time that this gold began to arrive, our railway trade increased immensely. Free trade was adopted, and enlarged our foreign trade; and our imports from China, as well as our outlay of capital in India, were doubled. Now, in China and India payments in silver only are accepted; this silver we purchase elsewhere with gold. These causes, along with an increase of our manufactures of trinkets, have taken up the extra quantity, so that a rise of about fifteen per cent. in prices is all that has occurred through the recent gold discoveries.

Did not the use of paper money prevent it, we should have, every now and then, to suffer by the changes of price which would arise from a sudden increase or decrease of the supply of gold. The credit which paper money represents steadies prices; for, when trade becomes good, more money is required for the increased business. That is at once found in the increased number of bills. When trade becomes bad, less money is needed. Fewer bills are then drawn or paid. Thus the money in circulation increases or diminishes as more commodities change hands in good trade, or fewer in bad; and a kind of steady balance is kept between commodities and money.

Paper money, when too plentiful, whether in notes or bills, causes what are called panics in trade—or commercial crises. Suppose that trade be good, bankers are ready to lend, and traders ready, perhaps too ready, to borrow, since high profits are being made, and, it is thought, will continue to be made. Then bills become plentiful, prices rise, and in the end they rise too high. People refrain from buying, there occurs a glut in the market—that is, there are now more goods than buyers, and merchants who had counted on paying their bills by the sale of goods, find that they cannot sell, and, therefore, cannot pay their creditors. These creditors in turn cannot pay theirs; and one after another, merchants fail in business. Trade becomes now as dull as it was before too active. Those who have money will not lend it to producers or speculators of any kind; they begin to withdraw it from the banks, and to distrust the value of the bank notes. They take them to the banks for the promised gold. Then occurs what is called a run on the bank. The one-third in gold of all they have promised in notes, which bankers find sufficient at an ordinary time, does not suffice in a panic. There is often not time enough allowed to send for more; the overstrained confidence of people has now turned to overstrained distrust; and simply through blind haste and fear, banks have been compelled to close, bankers been ruined, and depositors have lost a part, if not all, of their savings. It is sometimes said that such panics occur every nine years. They occur at any time after a period of too much credit and too extensive a circulation of bills. English history tells us of a fearful crisis of this kind in what is called the South Sea Bubble of 1720. In 1846 a railway mania brought ruin to many, and caused the value of the government funds to fall very much, as if the whole nation were about to become bankrupt.

To prevent such panics, if possible, the government

has passed a number of Acts restraining the powers of bankers in the issue of notes. The most important of these Acts is one passed in 1844. By it the Bank of England was allowed to issue fourteen millions of pounds in notes, because the property of the bank and the amount which government owed to it came to so much. For every one of these fourteen million pounds the bank could, therefore, beyond a doubt pay gold. If more notes were issued, then the bank was required to have gold in its cellars to the same amount. All other banks were forbidden to increase their issue of notes beyond what it had been during the year 1844; and no new banks were to be allowed to issue any. When any of the existing banks ceased from business, their issues were to be added to that allowed for the Bank of England. From this cause it now issues fifteen millions. Its notes can be changed for gold at any time, and so strong is the faith of the world in its ability to pay them in gold when required, that a Bank of England note is as readily received as gold in payment of goods or services in France, Germany, America, and in almost all the civilized world. The money in common use in a nation is called the **currency**. Paper money which by law can be changed for gold at any time is called a **convertible currency**; that which cannot, is called an **inconvertible currency**. In America there is an inconvertible currency; and the notes called greenbacks are of much less value than coins for the same nominal amount.

For any one to obtain credit he must be thought able to pay. The lender will not lend without some sort of **security**. This security may lie in the faith which the lender has in the faith of the borrower, or in his talent for business. Often the money is lent on the security of land which the borrower possesses. The lender receives the writings which give possession of this land till the borrower repays the money, and is paid the interest of the money, for years, it may be; the borrower all the time occupying the land. Such a mode of borrowing is called a **mortgage** of land or houses. Should the borrower become unable to pay the interest, and, of course, the whole sum borrowed, then the lender can take the property to himself, or sell it. This is called foreclosing a mortgage.

The **credit banks** of Germany are banks which lend on the security of the character of the borrower, and of that of his fellow-workmen who join with him in a promise to pay, as well as of their united business talent. In Scotland, the banks have a similar method of lending, not exactly to workmen, but to small traders, called **cash credits**. The Scotch banks receive deposits as low as ten pounds at a time. If a young man of good character and known business skill wishes to begin business for himself, and can find one or two friends of good credit who will become surety for him, up to a certain amount, the money is lent him by the bankers; not all at once, but in small sums as he requires them. He pays interest from day to day for what he borrows, and can from day to day return to the bank whatever money his business leaves him on hand, receiving interest on it. By this system many a man once poor, with, in fact, nothing but his good character, has raised himself to wealth. Thus, to act honourably when young, to be industrious and faithful, is the foundation of credit, and wins the power to use the savings of others in the making of one's own fortune. But not lightly will any one trust his savings, or give his security, to one who has never made any savings of his own. How will a man be careful of the property of others who is not careful of what he himself has earned? Those who would rise in life must begin by saving. The common banks of the country do not usually take a deposit of less than ten pounds, many of them not even that, and it is hard for a young man or woman to save up so much as could lead to an account with them. But there are, for such, **savings banks** in every town and post office, in which a shilling may be placed at a time. There is no need, then, for any one to wait long before **beginning an account, and every shilling put into a** savings bank begins at once to gain interest of about 2½ per cent. This is a small profit; but, as we know, large interest means heavy risk of loss. Money in the savings bank makes money, slowly but surely. There is no more risk of loss there than there is of the British nation becoming bankrupt. The habit of saving, once begun, is easy; the custom of spending odd pence and sixpences, because they are odd, is dangerous and keeps us always poor; while the feeling of having something laid past for a time of sickness, or by means of which we may secure some good position when it occurs, is in itself a pleasure greater than spending of petty sums can ever buy. The workman who has thus saved a little, and is for a time out of work, can afford to live for awhile upon his savings, and need not rush to the first poorly paid employment which turns up. He gains time to look about him; and what better means can there ever be of raising the wages of workmen, than by having workmen who need not, and will not, work for low ones?

Paper money, whether notes, bills of exchange, or cheques, increases the currency of a country in relation to the commodities, and therefore increases prices. The increase of gold from California and Australia has not greatly increased the prices of commodities.

Commercial panics arise from too much credit, followed by too little. By means of savings banks the poor may begin to accumulate wealth.

XXIV.—INSURANCE AND POOR LAWS.

WE have seen that one part of profit consists of payment for risk. Losses being certain—some time or other, to some one or other—men who run the risk of them, take advantage of what may be said to be one of the discoveries of modern times, that all events happen with a kind of uniformity. No man can tell what warehouses will take fire during the coming year, but that a certain number of those that exist will do so, is extremely probable. If then, all those who have warehouses or other buildings, the loss of which by fire they have reason to dread, subscribe a certain small sum, this can be paid to those who suffer the loss, and their loss repaired. Societies called **fire insurance societies** are formed, which offer, for a small yearly payment, called a **premium**, to make good the loss of any one who may suffer by fire. Such a society gains by the premiums of those whose places are not burnt, and loses by the value of those which are; and, by making the premiums of all insurers with them, taken together, a little higher than would be required to make good the loss of the number out of them likely to lose by fire, the society has a profit; those who suffer by fire are no worse than before, and the others lose only their small subscription.

The same kind of insurance is applied to the danger which foreign traders run of loss of ships and goods at sea. This is called **marine insurance**, and the men who for a premium undertake to make good the loss are called underwriters. In the same way, too, men insure in societies against **accidents**. Thus, by prudence and forethought, certain risks are lessened; but there is one evil, not merely a risk, which comes to all—death! To an individual death may be a gain, but to his wife and the family he leaves behind, it is certain loss—perhaps an unspeakable calamity. Prudence and forethought may serve to soften even this, for by means of **life assurance societies** each man may, if he will, provide something for those he loves in case of his sudden or early death. It is known how many men of every thousand now living are likely to die during the year, and even how many of each different age—of thirty, forty, or fifty years. The societies receive yearly premiums sufficient to pay all that is likely to be required, and leave a profit. Those who insure in youth pay smaller premiums than those who insure late in life; because the younger a man is, the likelier he is to live many years, and therefore he will pay a larger number of premiums before he dies. The families of those who die receive the sum assured; and those who live have, in the meantime, also gained in the ease of mind which springs from having provided for those dependent on them.

Loss by fire is only a possibility; death, sooner or later, is a certainty; and if it be prudent for all to provide against loss by fire, how much more is it for a man to insure for his family something to live upon in the case of his death. Few men of business neglect to do so; the number of workmen who do so is small, though every post office affords them an opportunity, with all the security our government can give, that the sum insured will be paid. Foolish and superstitious wives sometimes hinder them, under a notion that preparing against the heavy loss by a husband's death has something to do with causing that death. If workmen would only strive in their days of health to pay the premiums of life assurance, widows and orphans might often be saved from beggary and misery. To leave those to charity, whom a little forethought might have left able to help themselves, is a disgrace which no honourable man, however poor, would willingly incur.

Sickness, and the evils of old age, are also insured against by the wise and prudent. **Friendly societies**, some at least of which are well managed, give to the workman who joins them, and pays a small sum weekly or monthly, a wage during the time of ill health; and on his death, or that of his wife or child, a sum is paid to help the expenses of burial. Trades unions, so far as they effect this kind of insurance, are beneficial. In certain societies, and at every post-office, with the security of government, a man or woman may, by a small payment, yearly or monthly, secure, after he or she has attained old age, say sixty, a yearly salary or annuity; and thus on easy terms a means of living is provided for them when they have become too old to work.

In fact, if one comes to think of it, we spend our lives in effecting insurances. We insure when we provide for coming wants, or act so as to avoid coming dangers. By food, we insure against starvation; by clothes, against cold; by sleep, against fatigue. Nature takes care, by immediate pains, that we secure ourselves against these daily wants, but forethought is needful against evils that are sure to come, yet are not always present.

And what of those who are imprudent, and do not provide for future wants? They must suffer, unless charity steps in to relieve them. Now charity, to a right thinking man, is always a bitter draught. For what is charity but a taking of services from others and giving none in return? They who give it are good and kind, but they who receive it, even while they have their wants relieved, are humbled and put to shame. It is true that there are misfortunes which no man could foresee; and, to relieve these, charity comes like an angel from heaven; but even when it heals it hurts. When that great fire took place in the city of Chicago, and thousands were turned into the streets homeless and destitute, it was indeed a noble thing that the people of other cities—New York, London, Glasgow, Manchester—gave of their savings in charity to relieve the sufferers; but, would it not have been nobler still if it could have been truly said that every house had been insured, and that the insurance societies had paid the sufferers their due?

Charity, indeed, has its proper place in relieving those who do not suffer because of their own neglect and improvidence—in relieving children who have been deserted, and those who have been overwhelmed by sudden disaster against which no man could provide; but, disguise it as we will, it is the receiving of services and rendering none in return, and destroys the only true equality which can exist in society—that, by means of which the poorest is equal to the greatest—the giving of service for service.

Where charity is often received, the shame which it causes at first is apt to become dull; and many, rather than work, would prefer to live always upon charity. No greater curse can come upon a society than to have many in it who are quite content so to live. There are political economists who, seeing the evils of charity which is bestowed unthinkingly, how it degrades the receiver and leads to sloth, have said that whoever relieves a beggar does harm to society. That depends upon whether the wants relieved might, or might not, have been avoided by industry and forethought. But this is true, that a large number of our fellow-countrymen and countrywomen, who are strong and well able to work, look forward without shame to ending their days as receivers of public charity. "The parish," say they, "is bound to find us."

By this they mean that the rates called **poor rates** belong to them. These rates are local taxes, as we saw, levied under the authority of what are called **poor laws**. They support workhouses, houses for the poor, one perhaps in every large parish, or one to a number of small parishes united. Hence they are called union workhouses, or often, for shortness, unions.

These unions are unfortunately necessary, for the charity of private persons is, of course, only given at odd times, and in irregular sums; and the constant needs of the poor could never be so supplied. They provide for those whose labour has not been sufficient to keep them in youth, and to lay past for old age. But it is easy to see that poor laws, in making such a provision for the wants of labourers, have made it possible for them to work for smaller wages than they could otherwise have done. For where labourers are numerous and compete with each other, wages are sure to fall to what it is possible for the labourer to live on in the meantime. And what is spent on the workhouse is what should have been paid before as wages. Thus poor laws, even if they help to support the needy, help to make them needy. Since their effect is to make wages low, it is evident that those only who have wages to pay— namely, employers of labour, ought, in justice, to be made to pay poor rates. But these rates are levied upon everybody, even the labourers themselves; and thus skilful and careful workmen help the capitalist to pay that part of the wages of those who are careless, which is paid to them as inmates of the workhouse.

Then, again, where there are many poor, that is, mostly in large towns, these rates are very high. All rated buildings for workshops have much to pay, and therefore the cost of production of everything made in these workshops is increased. The goods are made dear there, and the makers of these goods in places where the poor rates are low can sell them cheaper; the consequence is that the trade of the over-taxed locality is ruined. From this cause, among others, it is said that the shipbuilding trade has been driven from London.

Charity is not due to those who have wasted and misspent their wages, as it is to those who suffer from unavoidable misfortune. The only way of preventing idlers from preferring charity to work is to make charity harder to them than work would be. This is what is attempted by the hard rules made for the poor in workhouses—the separation of husbands and wives, and the plain food that is alone given. Were it not so, the slothful would seek admission to them, and the industrious would be robbed, for their sakes, by high poor rates. Where, however, people are believed to be poor not by idleness or carelessness, an attempt is made to distinguish them from the idle and careless by giving them relief from the poor rates in their own homes.

If Political Economy has one lesson more important than another to teach, it is the duty of rendering service for service; and no man or woman does that who receives charity, whether from private hands, or by the orders of the law.

Insurance against loss by fire or other accidents, and life insurance, are duties which no one should neglect. He who neglects to provide as much as possible against future wants or misfortunes is likely to become an object of charity.

Charity is the receiving of services without giving any in return, and is rightly to be given only to those who suffer by unforeseen disasters.

XXV.—INTEMPERANCE.

"It is easy to save," a workman may say, "When one has plenty. If I had as good an income as my employer, I could save too, and would be glad enough to do so. How can working men save from such wages as they get?"

Now, in this, and in most civilized countries, it is not quite true that workmen can earn no more than is needed for their daily wants. And workmen have not all the same wages or the same expenses. There are some workmen who earn only a pound a week, others can make three or four. The married workman has three or four times the expenses of the unmarried. If, then, the man who is poorly paid, and the unmarried man, can live, there is no doubt that the man who is well paid, and the single man, could save. But the books of savings banks afford proof that it is not the workmen who are paid highest that save most; it is a known fact, too, that many well paid workmen save nothing at all, and yet neither keep their households in such comfort, nor educate their children so well, as others who have not half their wage and can still save a little. Such workmen live in a state in which the slightest misfortune—illness or loss of work for a couple of weeks—reduces them to be dependent upon charity, to ask for medical attendance gratis, to receive money from charitable visitors, and petty comforts from the pity of their neighbours. It is the families of such men that fill the workhouses and raise the poor rates. And one of the chief causes by which their high wages bring them neither comfort nor independence is this—they spend them on intoxicating drinks, such as beer, whisky, and gin.

The excessive use of wines and strong drinks is a vice which prevails too much among all classes; but most among working men. It is true that this vice is not now so common as it was in times gone by, when gentlemen used to boast of being drunk, and when it was no disgrace even to the highest statesmen to be seen reeling in the streets. But habits of economy, and a sense of self-respect, have led the higher classes as a whole to see the wastefulness and disgrace of intemperance; among the working men these habits and this sense have not the same sway. In the United Kingdom it is said that about thirty millions of pounds are spent yearly on spirits, and it will be hardly too much to count that twenty of these millions are spent by working people. In one city, we are told, there is a public-house for every fourteen families; and in a certain town, not long ago, there were 108 public-houses, and only 11 bakers' shops. In a town in France, of less than sixty thousand inhabitants, eighty thousand glasses of brandy are drunk in a day; and similar things might be related of every manufacturing town or city in Europe.

Of all other classes workmen should be the foes of intemperance. For, if it be true that the workman's wages amount to little more than yields the necessaries of life for him and his family, then, since liquor is no necessity of life, whatever he spends on that deprives him of so much of what is needful. Above all things it is a workman's interest to have cheap food. Now, in the making of spirits and ales large quantities of the chief kinds of food-products are destroyed. Barley, oats, wheat, rye, Indian corn, and potatoes are all, by well known chemical processes, used to produce alcohol, which is the main part of all kinds of spirits. The Russians, Turks, and Arabs make an alcoholic liquor out of milk. Now, if these things were sent to market as food, the price of food would no doubt be lower, and thus the working man's wage would be really increased, because it would go farther in the purchase of real nourishment for himself and his family. For, whatever be the pleasure

INTEMPERANCE.   131

which men derive from the use of spirits, the science of modern times has made it clear that they are not in any sense food. They pass through the body without being changed into any part of it; they help to form no part of bone, or muscle, or nerve, or any other organ of life. They simply excite, and in certain states make the action of the organs more energetic; but they no more afford nourishment than a crack of the whip nourishes the horse which for a moment it causes to gallop.

If it be the working man's interest to have food plentiful and cheap, it is no less so that the products in demand should be such as give most employment to labour, for the labourer's share in the price of such goods is greatest. The price of the raw material in cotton and woollen goods forms, as we have seen, but a small part of the whole cost of production, the greater part being payment for labour. Think of the number to whom a share of the ultimate price of cotton cloth is given, and who all receive benefit from the production of such goods, compared with the few who share in the ultimate price of spirituous liquors. In the one case we have the planters and their labourers, the seed-pickers, packers, shiploaders, shippers, and all others engaged in the transport of the raw cotton; then the carders, spinners, weavers, needle-women, and retailers,—all deriving a share of what the consumer of cotton goods pays. In the other, very few workmen are employed. Almost the whole cost of production of cotton cloth goes to the working class,—only about one-tenth of that of whisky or gin. The rest is paid chiefly as taxes. In the one case, we have a plant cultivated and made useful to mankind; in the other, good food destroyed. In the one case, even after the shirt, or whatever the article of cotton goods may be, has done its service to the consumer, it again enters on a new round of employment for labour in the form of rags, by means of which a whole host of rag-pickers, paper-makers, writers, engravers, printers, bookbinders, and others are made to yield pleasure and instruction to mankind, as well as profit to themselves; in the other, only a momentary pleasure at best is produced, which, too often, ends in pain and remorse. For, let it be granted that there is some pleasure in the use of spirits,—that the excitement they produce is agreeable, and in some cases necessary; yet, that excitement, as is well known, leads to a most painful re-action.

After a drinking bout, when the money is spent and the spirits consumed, what remains for the intemperate man to look upon as the result of his expense? Had he bought furniture or clothing for himself, his wife, and children; or had he bought pictures or household ornaments or books, then there would have remained, when the money was gone, the pride and pleasure of seeing his wife and children smart and comfortable, the gratification of a well-stocked house, the interest and instruction of the books. Pleasures such as these leave no sting behind; and they form a kind of capital for him, for out of them comes health of body and ease of mind, by means of which his daily toil is lightened, and his work made so much the better, for it is done under cheerful and happy influences.

And, then, it is not alone the price of the drink which is completely lost, but other sources of loss are joined to it. The workman who drinks a large part of his wages received on Saturday rarely goes to work on Monday. There are trades in which it is quite the usual thing not to work on Monday. Now see the loss. Let us suppose that a working man has only three shillings a day of wage, and the most of them have more; and let us suppose that from the age of twenty-one till that of forty-one, a period of twenty years, he wastes his Mondays in drinking and idling. He loses three shillings a week of wage, and he will hardly spend less than three shillings between Saturday and Monday on drink. That is, the sum of six shillings weekly goes for intemperance. Had he saved this six shillings during the time we have named, then, at the age of forty-one, still a comparatively young man, he would have had at his command a capital of above £300; considerably above it, if we count the interest it might have made. The task of those who seek to make workmen into capitalists by means of co-operation will prove a hard one, till the men can be induced to leave off the excessive use of spirits.

Here is another source of loss by drinking; it diminishes the workman's powers of production. It robs him of the power to use the workman's capital—namely, his health, skill, and character. How can the trembling hands of the drunkard do efficient work? How can his racked and muddled brain think out useful plans? Who could trust any enterprise requiring skill and energy and forethought to one of his unsteady habits? And there comes a time when the effects of excessive drinking make him quite incapable of doing even second rate work. Physicians in hospitals say that about a third of the cases of paralysis that are brought to them are caused by drink; and those in lunatic asylums reckon about one-seventh of the cases of madness as springing from the same cause.

Deadness of intellect is bad, but there comes yet a greater curse from intemperance—namely, hardness of heart and utter selfishness. In any manufacturing town one may, every Saturday night, see poorly clad mothers, and starved ragged children, following the husband and father, and vainly trying to get money from him. He has it, for it is pay-day; but, untouched by the misery of those he is bound to love and cherish, he means to spend it in the public-house. If, by their persistence in following him, he at last gives the mother something to buy food with, it is given with a growl and perhaps an oath. How of such workmen can capitalists be made?

It is true that these evils spring from the excessive use of intoxicating liquors; and it is possibly also true that a moderate use of them has some advantages. They may, rightly used, diminish the waste of the body, and they may enable us in a moment of need to make much greater exertions than we could make in ordinary moments. But there is always danger even in a moderate use of them—a danger which especially threatens the workman who is without much education. The peculiar pleasure they excite leads to a craving for its continuance, and this leads easily to the habit of using them. The habit once formed, it is scarcely possible to break off; and the result of it is almost every kind of suffering and crime.

Men have tried many ways of preventing intemperance. They have founded societies for total abstinence from the use of alcoholic liquors; they have made laws limiting the times and places at which such liquors could be sold, in some cases forbidding the sale of them entirely; and governments have imposed heavy taxes upon them. The societies, by means of which men encourage each other to voluntary total abstinence from their use, are more in agreement with the principles of political economy than any of the other remedies, and have been the means of greatly lessening the consumption of spirits in America and Great Britain. Laws to prevent the sale of intoxicating liquors are interferences with the freedom of trade; and, it is to be feared that, like all such interferences, they tend to raise up a class of smuggling traders in the place of those who would have dealt in them openly. Excessive taxes make liquors dear; and it was long ago pointed out by Adam Smith, whose writings raised political economy into a science, that when spirits are dear men have a pride in using them as a means of showing hospitality. "Nobody," says he, "affects the character of liberality and good fellowship by being profuse of a liquor which is as cheap as small beer." And this is certain, that where wines are cheap there is little or no excess in their use.

The best paid workmen do not save most money. Intemperance is the greatest hindrance to saving among the working classes.

The manufacture of spirits tends to make food dear, and gives little employment to labour. The excessive use of spirits destroys health and intellect, and hardens the heart. The moderate use of them is dangerous.

Societies for total abstinence are a better remedy for intemperance than laws forbidding the sale of liquors, or excessive taxes upon them.

XXVI.—DIVISIONS OF POLITICAL ECONOMY.

LET us look back now upon our past lessons. The subject we have been studying is **wealth**, how it is produced and how it is shared among the producers. We have learned that it is produced by **labour** and the **forces of nature**. We have seen that the results of labour are partly saved, and partly consumed by the producers. That which is saved and laid aside for the production of further wealth is **capital**, and gives rise to a division of the producers into those who have capital and those who have none. The first are **capitalists**, the second **labourers**. We have seen that in the division of the results brought about by the forces of **nature, labour, and capital**—or as some say, **land, labour, and capital**—the share got by nature is nothing; that got by labourers is **wages**; and that got by capitalists is wages, payment for **risk** of capital, and payment for their **abstinence** from the immediate use of capital. Again, we have learned that capital divides itself into two different parts, one of which, **fixed capital**, is used to make machines and tools whereby the forces of nature can be made to aid more efficiently in production; and roads, bridges, and railways, by which wealth can be more easily moved from place to place, and buildings in which it can be conveniently stored; the other, **circulating capital**, is that on which labourers subsist while they are engaged in the act of producing more wealth. We have seen, too, that the more of capital that is converted into fixed capital the less is left to support labour till such time as the action of the fixed capital has, by the help of natural forces, brought about a greater increase of wealth. All these, and the truths connected with them, form that part of Political Economy which concerns itself with the **laws of production.**

But Political Economy studies also how wealth is shared among the producers; that is, it studies the **laws of the distribution of wealth.** Now we have seen that the chief agent for distributing it when men are free is a mutual exchange of commodities on certain terms. But some portions of wealth are taken from men without their consent, such as **taxes.** Therefore, the study of the distribution of wealth divides itself into a study of **voluntary distribution,** that is, of exchange of wealth; and of **enforced distribution.** And this is what men really mean, when they say that **Political Economy** is the **science of the production, the exchange, and the distribution of wealth;** namely, that it is the science of the production, the voluntary distribution, and the enforced distribution of it.

In regard to voluntary distribution, or exchange, we learned that the great law is that of **service for service;** and that services are estimated under that other most important law of **supply and demand.** A service which is plentifully supplied, compared with the demand for it, has little or no value; a service which costs great trouble, and is scarce compared with the demand for it, is of high value. We have also seen that the services which cost trouble will not be produced for the purpose of exchange, unless the demand for them be such that the other services received in exchange for them form a sufficient reward for the trouble of producing them; that is, unless the price will pay the cost of production. We have studied, too, the different forms which the rewards given in exchange for different kinds of services assume, such as **wages, profits, rents,** and **hire,** and how the law of supply and demand affects each of them. We learned also something of what may be called the artificial mechanism of voluntary distribution or ex-

DIVISIONS OF POLITICAL ECONOMY. 137

change, when we studied the nature of **banking agencies,** of bank notes, bills of exchange, and cheques, and their effects in bringing about a rise or fall of prices. And we learned of that wondrous natural mechanism of exchange, **competition,** by which everything that can be produced is brought to the place of exchange, the market, at the lowest possible price—the cost of production. So far as the laws of voluntary distribution are concerned, these were the main subjects of study.

In what is usually called **distribution,** or as it should be more exactly described, **enforced distribution,** we studied the **nature of taxes,** the rules to which they should conform, their different divisions, and the more special effects of some of them, such as the **poor rates.** We have seen the evil of enforced **monopolies,** and have learned the injustice of the attempts which were once so commonly made by our laws to compel consumers at home to give more of their wealth than was needful to home producers; and have learned, too, the wondrously beneficial results that have come to society since our lawgivers learned to let commerce alone, to allow foreigners to bring us their produce as they please, and so suffered the bounties of nature, to other more favoured climes, to spread over our own land freely.

One lesson which cannot fail to impress itself upon all who attentively study such subjects is the great advantage to society of voluntary distribution, and the disadvantage of enforced distribution. When governments insist upon monopolies and protection laws, and when either governments or societies of workmen try to enforce a certain rate of wages, capital is apt first to take fright, then flight, from the scene of such enforcements. It is a lesson to rulers and subjects alike, that freedom is the best safeguard of plenty; before the oppression, and even before the too active interference of either kings or people, famine is apt to stalk, although their interfering measures may be taken with the best of intentions. The untrammelled freedom of mankind to work out what their own interests require, produces wealth far more surely than the best individual direction, for the sense of all mankind is greater than that of any one lawgiver.

Under a rule of free exchange, each man, it is true, looks after his own interests; but he does not thereby injure those of others. "One man's gain is another man's loss," is the rule in gambling, but not in trade. Here is a shoemaker who wants a hat, and has a pair of shoes unsold beside him. There is a hatter who wants shoes, and has plenty of hats. These two meet, talk, learn each other's wants, and make an exchange. Each of them has gained what he wants and neither has lost. A hat and a pair of shoes have changed owners. One man's gain has been another's profit. The shoemaker and the hatter represent all commerce.

Nations have always made progress in wealth as they progressed in commercial freedom, and declined as it declined. The kingdom of Spain sank low, the republics of Carthage and Venice sank altogether, under a load of prohibitions. Great Britain has risen higher commercially every day since hers were taken off. The Emperor Napoleon I. was wont, in his days of exile, to say that he dated his fall and the misfortunes of France from the day on which he signed the Decrees of Berlin, forbidding all commerce between Great Britain and the rest of Europe. "I felt," he said, "in the act of signing my name, that there would be no more repose for me."

Political Economy is usually divided into three branches, production, exchange, and distribution of wealth. The last two would be more properly called free and enforced distribution of wealth.

The great lesson of the whole science is, that commerce should be left free from oppressive restrictions by governments on the one hand, and by unions of workmen on the other.

XXVII.—THE OBJECT OF POLITICAL ECONOMY.

WE have thus learnt something of the general principles of Political Economy, and of the advantages of freedom for the working out of these principles in increasing the wealth of society. We have learnt, too, some matters of detail in regard to the nature of labour, which it is important that we should keep in recollection. Capital and labour, we saw, are not essentially different in their nature; they are the forces which must work together, with the forces of nature, in the production of goods and services. Capital is the work of yesterday and of all past days, whose produce has not been consumed, but remains embodied in commodities for the use of other labour. Labour is the work of to-day. Capital and labour then differ in regard to time, but not in other respects. And as there are two kinds of **capital, circulating** and **fixed,** there are two kinds of **labour, skilled** and **unskilled.** The one, mere manual labour, is the exercise of strength alone; the other is the exercise of strength, together with intelligence. If it be right to speak of manual labourers as "hands," it would not be wrong to speak of skilled labourers as "heads." We saw, in our lessons, that the heads earn more than the hands, and we found the justification of this in the fact that intelligence is scarcer and more in demand than strength; that iron can supply strength to almost any amount, while only education, and that rare gift of nature, genius, can supply the intelligence which society prizes and pays for. And society prizes and pays for it, not through any desire to set one man above another, but because the services of the man who applies intelligence to labour, who uses his inventive faculties, are so much greater in their amount than those of the mere manual labourer. A porter, with a rope and a basket, can carry but a small weight to no great distance in a day; let him apply to his labour the intelligence necessary to construct a wheelbarrow, instead of a basket, and he will easily convey twice as heavy a load to twice the distance. But let any one apply the still greater amount of intelligence necessary to break and use a horse, he may then easily convey a burden as heavy as that he could carry in his barrow to six times the distance in a day, and thus do twenty-four times the work of the porter with his basket. Let him still further employ the intelligence needful to invent a cart, and yoke the horse to it, the burden may then be doubled, and his day's work will be forty-eight times that of the porter with his basket. Still further, let intelligence be ever more and more applied to this business of carrying burdens, so that at last a railway is laid, and locomotives and carriages built, then two men, a fireman and a conductor, may convey easily ten thousand times as much as one porter to twenty times the distance in a day. That is, these two could do two hundred thousand times the work of one man, or each of them one hundred thousand times as much. And all this extra rendering of services is what comes of the application of intelligence and invention to labour—of labour being skilled.

Consider also—for we cannot learn the truth too well, that it is intelligence, not mere labour, which does efficient work—consider the arrangement of parallel rods, which may be seen at the end of the beam of any steam engine. It is an arrangement contrived by James Watt to keep the piston moving straight up and down in the cylinder, while it gives an up and down circular motion to the beam. There is, perhaps, no finer bit of intelligent arrangement in all our varied machinery. And without it, men might have had all the rest of the machine, iron, boiler, coals, everything, but it would not have moved so as to render them efficient service.

It is right, then, as we have seen, that those who first apply any peculiar form of intelligence to labour should have an ample reward. They generally get it by the patents which allow them the sole right to the use of their inventions for a time; and, truly, they are worthy of it. For notice this, though nature does her work for nothing, it is because she is forced to do it by the arrangements or inventions which skilled workmen make. The harvests do not grow up of themselves; water will grind no corn unless men make wheels for it to drive; steam will drive no machinery unless labour and intelligence unite to compel it by an arrangement of pistons, valves, and beams. In the face of nature, man with strength and without intelligence is the most helpless of beings. And who can number the long ages during which men, with their intellects as yet but weak, strove hard against the harshness of nature, working with flint tools, till intelligence grew, and they saw the way to cast and work metals, and in the end to force from the soil, and the waters, and the air, the rich services they now render us? Men's arms were strong enough during these long ages—nay stronger, some think—than ours are now; for savages, generally, are stronger than civilized men. The success of the men of to-day, in making nature work for them, has been gained, not by strength, but by intelligence. Let those workmen, then, who by the application of intelligence to their work, bring out inventions, and so richly multiply the produce of human labour, have their rewards ungrudged, by patents, till some better way of rewarding them be found. And, doubtless, there might be a better way. For, as we have seen, it is not always the real inventor who receives the reward which it is meant that a patent should confer. But let us notice this, that invent as they will, still it is society as a whole which ultimately receives the whole benefit of their labours in increased production and cheapness of commodities; for these patents, and the monopolies they confer, expire after a few years, and any one may then use the invention in the production of goods and services.

Now, this increased production of commodities, and greater cheapness, by means of which a wider distribution of them is caused, are the very objects at which Political

Economy as a science may be said to aim. Every science worthy of the name has two parts: one, in which it studies laws, called its theoretical part; another, in which it applies these laws to practice, endeavouring to produce some material good for society, or to increase the power of mankind over nature. This is its practical part. The theoretical part of Political Economy is, as we have seen, the study of the laws and distribution of wealth; the practical part—the material good which it seeks to aid in effecting—is the making of men's labour more productive, and the spread of the increased produce over the greatest possible number of men. For this end, it shows the advantages of freedom in commerce, the uses of machinery, the fallacy of such proposals as those of Communism and Socialism, and the evil as well as injustice of many of the proceedings of trades unions. Its practical object is really the same as that of Communists and trades unions is pretended to be—namely, the giving of greater wealth to all; and, indeed, since all reasonable men are workers in one form or other, its object, more strictly than theirs, is an increase of wages to all. But it does not seek to effect its object as they do, by robbing capital of its interest and profits. It teaches that, to rob capital of its profits, is the sure way to destroy it, by taking away the motive to save, and will thus lead in the end to general poverty.

How then, it may be asked, can this object be effected, —how is it possible for a rise of wages to be brought about without a lessening of the profits of capital? By means of the principle we have just learned,—that increased intelligence applied to labour may increase to any extent the products of that labour; and that the beneficial results of increased intelligence come always in the end to society, and cost it nothing. Inventions become ultimately free for every one to use in production. Of the three producers of all goods and services, capital must always be paid, or it would not be saved; labour must always be paid, for workmen must eat and have wherewithal to be clothed; but nature is not paid. And now we see that the main part of efficient labour—intelligence or invention—works also, after a time, without payment. Who pays anything to inventors to be allowed to use a cart, or a spade, or a wheelbarrow, or a printing-press, or a spinning-jenny, or even a railroad or a locomotive, unless there be some special recent improvement in its structure? We pay nothing now for inventions that are a quarter of a century old; in less than another quarter of a century every patented machine that has now to be paid for will be producing its work for nothing.

This, then, is the answer of Political Economy to the question, How can wages be raised, and profits not be diminished? By the increased efficiency of inventions in production; by the use of more work of machinery, and less of that of men; and by the consequent greater amount of production, and the larger sum which can be distributed as wages. The more society progresses, the greater is the share of nature and invention—these unpaid workers—in the production of commodities, and the less the need for human labour; while the quantity of the products that can satisfy human wants becomes always greater. So that the very objects—namely, less work and higher wages—which trades unions seek to effect by their clumsy and often cruel arrangements, and which they do not effect, are shown to be the sure result of the wondrous and silent operation of the laws which govern both human and material nature.

There is one thing of which we may now be certain: that, where wages have risen suddenly without an increase of productive power,—that is, of the means to pay them,—they cannot long remain high. If they have risen at the expense of capital, that capital will soon be withdrawn from trade; if they have risen at the expense of consumers,—by an increase of the prices of goods,— then the goods which are thus made dear, being liable to competition of workmen and producers in other countries, will be produced, in all probability, cheaper by them, and the result will be the ultimate loss of work, instead of higher wages. There is but one safe ground for higher wages—increased productive power; and that comes from the application of skill and science to labour.

And so Political Economy urges its lessons upon all of us, often without being heard, and under unmerited reproach. Men who know little of it, speak of it as if its doctrines destroyed the feelings of humanity, led to the abolition of charity, set up mutual grinding by competition, and freed every man from being his brother's keeper; while the truth is, that it seeks to lessen human suffering and increase human comforts, to show governments how to make their subjects richer in the means of life; and bodies of men where what they seek is impossible of attainment, or can be attained in better ways. For many years it pled with society for freedom of commerce, and in vain. When, at last, its teachings were listened to, burdens upon commerce removed, and free trade adopted, they were justified even beyond the expectations of its wisest teachers. Since then the wages of workmen have risen; and although, of course, the prices of dairy and farm produce have also risen since the demand of a wealthier population has caused an increase of such produce, always at a greater cost of production; yet the increased cheapness of manufactured goods, which are always cheaper the greater the demand, has more than atoned for the rise of agricultural products.

And now that Political Economy seeks to be heard between the contending ranks of capital and labour, we may safely say that their disputes can only be rightly settled when its conclusions are adopted, and higher wages sought, not in strikes and limitation of the number of apprentices, but in increased production by means of more intelligent labour.

It will be well, too, when individuals will try and carry out its doctrines as far as these concern themselves. To a workman who clearly understands them, there are certain of its truths which cannot fail to come home. He will know better than to believe that those only work who work with their hands; and will respect intelligence, whether it be shown in the results of scientific study, or in the care and skill of the foreman under whose direction he labours. He will know better than consider the successful capitalist as a mere grinder of labourers, and will see in him, instead, the man by whose acuteness and foresight new markets are opened up, and new kinds of goods brought forward; whose multiplied schemes are, in reality, multiplied means of work and wage for him and his fellow-workmen. He will know that there is but one means for himself of sharing in the profits of capital—that is, by saving; and will consider that no saving can be too petty since all help to such an end. He will know the advantage of never purchasing except by ready money, since this makes him careful of his expenses, and will avoid debt and the pawnshop like the gates of doom. Knowing the value of freedom in trade, he will be careful how he connects himself with societies which limit his own right and that of his neighbour to work when, and where, and for what, he pleases; nor will he readily become a party to such an organization of labour as would deprive him of the benefit of his own skill, by arranging that all workmen of the same trade should have the same wage without respect of industry or ability. Such a man will readily understand and seek the peace of mind which life assurance is calculated to yield; will know how it is that trustworthiness as well as skill tend to make workmen valuable, and raise their wages; and will rightly estimate the value of temperance as a means of that happiness, and health, and intelligence, which enables a man to work well, and which wins the respect and confidence of neighbours and employers.

Capital and labour are, in effect, the same thing. The one is the work of the past embodied in commodities saved for future production; the other is the work of the present time.

Intelligence is the most essential part of really productive labour. In the form of invention it works, like nature, for nothing.

The object of Political Economy is the increase and spread of wealth.

K

XXVIII.—PROTECTION: THE MAYOR OF ENIOS; AN ILLUSTRATION.

The following story is one of the many pleasant illustrations of the absurdity of protectionist theories which are to be found in the works of Bastiat, a famous French writer on Political Economy:—

"At the time when the people of Paris were seeking mines of asphalte among the Pyrenees mountains, with the intention of working them, the chief magistrate of Enios,—a commune, or small township in France, entertained a traveller for some days. This stranger,—when he went away, forgot to take with him two or three numbers of the newspaper called the *Industrial Monitor*. Naturally, the mayor glanced over them, and became interested in what he read. 'Truly,' cried he, 'here is a newspaper writer who knows a thing or two. Forbid, protect, keep out, restrain, prohibit. Ah! there's a system; it is as clear as daylight. I have always said that our people would be ruined, if the exchange of goods were left completely free ; we have not enough of protectionist laws in France. We prohibit goods on the frontiers of the country, it is true ; but why do we not prohibit them on the borders of every commune? Why should we not be consistent and logical?'

"Now, the chief magistrate of Enios was no theorist, and could find neither peace nor rest till he had communicated to all his fellow-magistrates the new notions that were buzzing in his head.

"The nature of the locality around Enios was wondrously adapted for the carrying out of his plans. Enios is separated from the rest of France, on the one side by inacessible rocks, on the other by an impassable torrent. A single bridge, thrown across the raging stream, is the only means of communicating with the world beyond.

"The mayor assembled his council. 'My friends,' said he, 'you know that the bridge has cost us no small sum. We had to borrow money to make it, and we have still the interest to pay, as well as the principal. I am going, for this very reason, to impose upon you an additional tax.'

"JEROME—'What, is the toll not enough?'—'A good system of tolls, sir,' said the chief magistrate, 'should have in view not the revenue, but protection. So far, the bridge has paid itself; but I intend us to arrange so that it won't bring any more revenue in the shape of toll dues. In fact, all our own goods will be carried away without payment of toll, and those of the commune on the other side of the river will not come in here at all.'

"JACQUES—'And what profit will that be?'—'Look, now,' said the mayor, 'would you not be very glad if the folks of Enios would pay you a little more for your butter.'—'Certainly,' said Jacques.—'Well, then, to bring that about, we must hinder the butter of other communes from getting in. And you, John, why is it that you are so long in making a fortune out of your poultry?'

" 'Because I have to sell them for so little,' said JOHN.—'You will see then,' said the mayor, 'the advantage of keeping those of other communes out of our market. My friends, what is ruining us is the in-bringing of foreign produce. Is it not perfectly just that our own town market should be kept for our own town workmen? Whether you speak of dairy or field produce, or of wine, are there not other communes more productive than ours in every one of these? And shall these come here and take away our own work from us? That is not competition, it is a monopoly which they possess. Let us take means, each helping the other, to make ourselves independent of them.'

"PETER THE CLOG-MAKER.—'At this very moment I am in want of oil, and nobody makes it in our commune.'—'Oil ! Why, our shale rocks are full of it. All we have to do is to extract it. There will be a new source of work for us—and work is wealth. Peter, don't you see that this confounded foreign oil causes us to lose all the wealth that nature has stored up in our own shales.'

"THE SCHOOLMASTER.—'But while Peter is grinding the shale rock, he can't be making clogs. If he can get more oil in the same time and with the same trouble by grinding the rocks than he can by making clogs, then your tariff will be useless. But if, on the contrary, he can get more oil by making clogs than by grinding slates, it will be hurtful. We have at present the choice of the two ways. Your plan will reduce us to one only, and very likely the worst one. It is not enough merely that there should be oil in the rocks; it must also be shown to be worth all the trouble necessary to extract it ; and more, that the time so spent could not be better employed at some other kind of work. What harm can there be in leaving us our choice of the two ways?'

"This kind of reasoning puzzled the chief magistrate; but then he bethought himself of an unanswerable argument. 'Monsieur the Schoolmaster,' said he, 'I command you to be silent, and I dismiss you from your office.'

"But these fine notions of local government, these profound views of social economy, were soon talked of at the offices of the prefect or governor of the district, and the protectionist tariff of the commune of Enios was disallowed at once by the government. The mayor hastened to the capital of the district, and valiantly defended his system. Then occurred between the prefect and the chief magistrate the strangest discussion ever heard. The prefect, we should know, was a red hot protectionist also ; so that every argument he used for general custom-house duties was turned by the mayor in support of his own local tariff at the bridge of Enios.

" 'What,' said the prefect, 'you want to hinder the cloth of the neighbouring communes from being brought into Enios?' —'You hinder the cloth of other countries from entering France,' said the chief magistrate. 'That is a different thing ; I wish to protect the national industry.'—'And I wish to protect the industry of my commune.' 'Is it not just that the French legislative body should defend French fabrics against foreign competition?'—'Is it not just that the municipality of Enios should defend the fabrics of Enios against the competition of neighbouring communes?' 'Monsieur the mayor, you presume too far, and I am not responsible to you in any way. In the meantime I order the resolution respecting the tariff at Enios to be set aside altogether.'

"The mayor took the road homeward a sadder, but scarcely a wiser man. He grumbled against men who use two sets of weights and measures ; and the people of Enios continued to buy from neighbouring communes such goods as they could not manufacture so well and so cheaply at home.

"All this confirmed their chief more and more in his opinion, that men are naturally inclined to ruin themselves, if they only have the misfortune to be free."

EXERCISES ON THE LESSONS.

1. What objects do men seek to attain by labour? What is the law which binds society? What is the object of the study of political economy? What would be the result of each man making his own house furniture?

2. How can one honestly obtain a loaf without purchase or gift? In what does the value of an article consist? Is sunlight an object of value? Is a sermon an object of value?

3. What is barter? Show the difficulty of trade between a butcher, a shoemaker, and a mason, by means of barter alone. Give some reasons for the use of gold and silver as money. What is wealth? Can there be a general rise of values? Can there be a general rise of prices? What is meant by a double standard of value?

4. What are the two agents in the production of wealth? What is it that is paid for when goods are bought? What is meant by cost of production? What kinds of trades are highly paid? Why?

5. Why is mental labour paid higher than manual labour? What did Malthus teach? How is it that a large population diminishes wages? What checks have been proposed to limit over-population? What is emigration?

6. State five advantages of the division of labour. In what cases are small farms good? In what cases are large ones good? What is a lease? What is Ulster tenant-right? How does division of labour apply to different countries?

7. What is capital, as distinct from savings? What is the wages fund? Do high prices of goods cause high wages? What is a glut of capital?

8. What is circulating capital? What is fixed capital? Can capitalists fix the rate of wages? What would be the effect of a law fixing wages at a high rate?

9. Of what elements does profit consist? What are the funds? Explain the dealings of speculators in the funds, and in shares of joint-stock companies. How do speculations in corn affect its price?

10. What are interest, freight, hire, and rent? How is their rate made higher and lower? What is usury? What is the effect upon borrowers of a law forbidding it?

11. What evil is usually done to labourers by the invention of machinery? State some of the advantages of machinery? What is the best preventive of loss of work by machinery?

12. Whether does a miser, or a prodigal, or a capitalist most benefit society? Is all luxury bad? Give examples of things of daily use which were once considered luxuries. How can justifiable luxury help to raise wages?

13. How is the price of goods, of which it is quite impossible to increase the quantity, fixed in the market? How is the price of agricultural produce fixed? How is that of manufactured goods fixed? What is the natural price? What is the market price of goods?

14. What is the foundation of the right of property? What is Communism? What would be the effect upon society of an equal distribution of property? What is St. Simonism? Fourierism?

15. What is rent? What is the nature of land as a marketable commodity? If rents were taken from landowners, would it make the price of corn less? What is the Metayer system of rents?

16. What capital may be said to be invested in a workman? What are the effects of education in regard to the efficiency of labour? Describe the mode of learning and practising a trade in the olden time. What are the effects of long apprenticeships?

17. What is competition? What are monopolies? What is the difference between producers and consumers in regard to competition? Name the articles monopolized in the time of Queen Elizabeth. How may over-competition be regulated?

18. Describe a trades union and its objects. What is a strike? What is a lock-out? Whether can masters or workmen endure longest in a struggle? Show the effects of a law reducing the hours of labour.

19. What are boards of arbitration? What are co-operative stores? Where is co-operation chiefly applied to the production of goods? In what way is co-operation applied in Germany? What are industrial partnerships? What are the chief good, and the chief bad, points of co-operation?

20. What are taxes paid for? What are the chief rules to which taxation should conform? How may taxes be divided? What is the difference between direct and indirect taxation? What is the effect of a tax on raw materials? What is the amount of the national debt?

21. What are export duties? What are import duties? What is their object? What were the chief arguments of protectionists for such duties? Is it possible for a country to be altogether independent of foreigners? What are patents? What is copyright?

22. What are the chief uses of banks? Whence come a

banker's profits? What are bills of exchange? What are accommodation bills? What are cheques and letters of credit? What is done at the clearing-house?

23. What is the effect of bank-notes, bills, and cheques upon the prices of commodities? What has been the effect upon prices of the recent importation of gold from California and Australia? Describe the course of a commercial crisis. What are cash credits? What are the advantages of savings banks?

24. Describe the nature of fire insurance. What is life insurance? What is marine insurance? What is an underwriter? What is an annuity? What is the object of the poor laws? What is the nature of charity, as viewed by the teachings of political economy?

25. Why should workmen especially be foes of intemperance? Show the difference in results to the working classes between expenditure on cotton or linen goods, and on beer, whisky, or gin. Do ardent spirits nourish the body? To what losses, besides that of money, does a habit of intemperance lead? Do excessive taxes upon liquors tend to diminish intemperance?

26. What are the divisions of political economy? Explain these divisions, and state some of the truths which fall under each.

27. In what respect do capital and labour differ? Show the importance of intelligence in regard to labour. To whom do the benefits of inventions ultimately fall? Can wages be raised without diminishing the profits of capital? Under what circumstances can a sudden rise of wages be lasting?

MISCELLANEOUS EXERCISES.

I.

1. What is the standard measure of value?
2. How do shipbuilders and sailors help to produce food and clothing?
3. What do men live upon while they are farming, cooking, manufacturing, and building?
4. How do weavers and tailors help to build ships and houses?
5. What do builders and engineers live upon while they are learning their trades?
6. How do miners, smiths, and cutlers help to produce food, clothing, and shelter?

7. What must men practise besides industry, before they can produce much wealth?
8. How do dishonesty and disorder in society prevent the production and accumulation of wealth?
9. What is co-operation?
10. By what division of labour does the editor of a newspaper assist in the better paving and lighting of a town?
11. By what division of labour do bakers, butchers, and tailors assist to convey passengers by rail?
12. Why do men strive to acquire skill?
13. How does protection of property encourage industry, skill, and economy?
14. Why is some capital called "circulating," and some "fixed"?
15. Does fixed capital increase more than circulating as civilization advances? Why?
16. What is a capitalist?
17. When large capitals are required to perform great works, and there are no large capitalists in a country, how can the great works be carried out?
18. When a tradesman has only a small capital, and receives an order, to fulfil which requires large capital, what must he do?
19. What are wages paid out of?
20. Why are some capitalists obliged to pay higher wages than others?
21. Can lowness of wages be prevented? How?
22. In which country will people be most industrious—where the increase of population is limited by want, or by fear of want?
23. What capital must a miller possess besides his mill?
24. Why are the summits of mountains not cultivated?
25. Why will land in one situation obtain for its owner a larger rent than an equal extent of land of the same quality in another situation?
26. How can borrowers afford to pay interest?
27. What causes the market value of a commodity to rise?
28. What is the limit below which the market value of a commodity will not fall?
29. How does the prospect of a large supply, as of a coming good harvest, affect the price of corn?
30. Some commodities are necessaries of life; others are luxuries. Of which will the value be most increased when the supply begins to fail?
31. If the market value of any commodity greatly exceed the cost of production, what will be the consequence?
32. If the market value of any commodity be greatly below the cost of production, what will follow?
33. What is the standard measure of value? Of price?

MISCELLANEOUS EXERCISES.

34. Do silver and gold always maintain the same value in relation to each other?
35. Are people in this country allowed to pay what they owe in gold or silver, as they think most to their own advantage?
36. What would be the effect on the value of gold and silver by the discovery of new and rich mines of both?
37. What would be the effect on the value of gold and silver if all bank-notes were recalled by the bankers?
38. In what way would a rise or fall of the value of either gold or silver show itself?
39. What would be the effect of a large addition to the supply of gold upon the price of corn?
40. How does a rise in the price of a commodity lead to a further supply of it?
41. When speculators are right in their calculations respecting coming prices, does society benefit in common with them?
42. In what way can the inhabitants of America and England best procure for their common benefit an abundant supply of food?
43. How do retail dealers add to the cost of production of goods?
44. What advantage do their customers get for this addition to the price of goods?
45. How might the customers avoid this extra price?
46. What is an intermediary?
47. Why are 112 separate pounds of sugar more valuable than one cwt.?
48. Show how competition may lower prices.
49. Show how competition can raise prices.
50. What is it that really lowers or raises prices?
51. What is it that really lowers or raises profits?
52. What is it that really lowers or raises wages?
53. What is credit?
54. How is foreign trade conducted without much use of money?
55. What is paper money?
56. In what way can a bank-note for £5 become less valuable than five sovereigns?
57. What is meant by currency?
58. How do the issuers of paper money make a profit by their issues?
59. How does paper money promote exchange?
60. What was ordered by the Bank Act of 1844?
61. What is meant by the *par* of exchange?
62. Is the exchange always at par? Why not?
63. When is the exchange above par?
64. Some countries always export the precious metals; some always import them. Why?

65. If the market prices of *all* commodities in Great Britain were to rise above the market prices in all other countries, what would happen?

66. What effect would be produced on prices by an extensive export of gold and silver?

67. What is freight? How much higher will the prices of commodities be in the countries which import them, than the prices of the same commodities in the countries which export them?

68. What is meant by inconvertible paper money?

69. How can a convertible bank-note be of less value than it represents?

70. What is meant by the price of gold?

71. How do insurance companies aid in preventing destitution?

72. How do municipal governments aid in the same?

73. How do general governments aid in this?

74. What effect will a rise of rents have on the land previously under cultivation?

75. How may the rent of land continually increase without any rise of prices?

76. What effect will a rise in the price of raw materials have on the cultivation of land that was before uncultivated?

77. In what kind of country are rents the highest?

78. What is the difference between real wages and money wages?

79. How can we compare correctly the wages of workmen in distant places, or in different periods?

80. How would debasement of current coin—that is, mixing the gold or silver with more plentiful metals—affect a workman's money wages?

81. How would it affect his real wages?

82. How are profits estimated?

83. How does it happen that the rate of interest is often spoken of as the price of money?

84. How can one borrower afford to pay a rate of interest which another cannot?

85. What causes the rate of interest in one country to differ from that in another?

86. What are the advantages of bridges, highways, mills, docks, canals, and insurance?

87. By what arrangements are the idle, drunken, and wasteful enabled to live in the midst of a civilized people?

88. What is government?

89. What services do men who hold government situations render to society?

90. What is a customs-tax? An excise-tax? An income-tax?

91. What are assessed taxes?

92. What is a smuggler?

MISCELLANEOUS EXERCISES.

93. By what name are local taxes generally known?
94. From whom do custom-house officers receive duties?
95. From whom do excise officers receive duties?
96. Those who seem to pay them really pay them. Is this true of direct or indirect taxes?
97. How may a man avoid paying the tax on tobacco?
98. How may a man avoid paying part of his income-tax?
99. What is the effect of a tax upon the price of the commodity taxed?
100. Compare hoarding, by merely depositing in a bank, with hoarding as practised in olden times by misers.

II.

1. "Land, labour, and capital are the sources of wealth," it is sometimes said. What is the payment of labour? Of capital? Of land? What other things must be included under the term "land"?
2. What regulates the current rate of interest? What regulates the price of any manufactured commodity?
3. What regulates wages in any special branch of industry? What effects have strikes and trades unions on wages? On what principles have unions of employers been formed?
4. What are the advantages of protective duties? Do prohibitive duties always produce their intended effect?
5. What are the common coins now used? What is meant by value, price, currency, standard of value?
6. What constitutes the original right of property? On what principles is this right transferred? What connection is there between the tenure of land and its productiveness?
7. Explain the difference between rates and taxes. Describe the different rates to which a man is liable who lives (1.) in the country; (2.) in a borough.
8. Show the advantages of division of labour.
9. Economy adds to the capital of the country; and capital is the fund which pays wages. Explain this.
10. What were the Jewish laws about lending money? Is it reasonable to treat money in a different manner from other commodities?
11. What is the origin of the payment of rent for land? What is a lease? Why are leases beneficial to tenants?
12. Point out the fallacy in this assertion, "Labour alone makes things valuable."
13. What artificial means have been employed to raise the rate of wages? With what effect on (1.) employers? (2.) workmen?
14. What are the conditions essential to the creation and preservation of wealth in a state? How does accumulated wealth promote the prosperity of a community?

15. Are accumulation and diffusion of wealth necessarily inconsistent with each other?

16. Explain the terms "Bills of exchange," "Drafts payable to order," "Cheques," "Accommodation bills."

17. Give remarkable instances of the number of persons employed in producing articles of no great value.

18. Whether is luxurious expenditure or hoarding most pernicious to society?

19. What would be the probable consequences of a redistribution of the wealth equally among all the citizens?

20. "The first object of government is to secure to every citizen security of life and property." How is this object secured in this country?

21. What is the difference between natural price and market price?

22. Show that wealth is the result of labour, hence that greater produce from less labour is the aim of all improvement. How does this affect the policy of trades unions?

23. In what way is the competition of traders beneficial to the consumer? What is the general effect of monopoly?

24. What would be the effect of laws to fix (1.) the price of provisions? (2.) wages? (3.) interest?

25. "The diversity of productions in the different countries of the world is the primeval law which sanctions exchange." Explain this; give instances. What is meant by the balance of trade between two countries?

26. Show that all legislation on the subject of commerce should proceed on the principle of considering the interest of the consumer before that of the producer.

27. "Every prodigal is a public enemy; and every frugal man a public benefactor." Explain this.

28. Explain the law of "Supply and demand."

29. Explain fully the nature of a bank-note.

30. What are the effects of a poor law?

31. Explain and judge the worth of "Reciprocal free trade"?

32. Is the national debt an advantage to the community? How much of every pound paid in taxes is applied to pay the interest of it? What is its amount?

33. What are the qualities which render gold and silver a good medium of exchange? What would be the effect of making both gold and silver legal tenders?

34. What is the difference between direct and indirect taxation?

35. Define property. What is meant by Socialism? Communism? Competition? Co-operation?

36. Why are a spade, a silver spoon, a poem, a dog, things of value? Show that there cannot be a universal rise of values.

37. Point out the fallacy of the old doctrine, "that the foreign

trade of a country is in a healthy condition only when the exports exceed the imports."

38. What determines the market value of labour? Has the price of provisions any direct influence on the payment for labour?

39. What is meant by the terms "Productive labourers"? "Unproductive labourers"? "Productive capital"? "Unproductive capital"? "Productive consumption"? "Unproductive consumption"?

40. What was the mercantile system?

41. Why should one not give alms to a sturdy beggar?

42. Which is more profitable, a large or a small scale of production? *(a)* in manufactures? *(b)* in agriculture?

43. In which class of taxes—the direct or the indirect—is the temptation to evade payment the strongest?

44. How do customs duties, excise duties, and direct taxes affect industrial operations?

45. State fully the advantages of machinery.

46. Capital is meant to be destroyed in the using. Explain this; and show the difference in reference to fixed and circulating capital.

47. "One man's gain is another's loss." Does this apply to commercial pursuits?

48. Explain the nature of a joint-stock company.

49. What are patents and copyrights?

50. "My wife, my child, my house, my farm." Is the same right of property implied in all these uses of the word "My"?

DEFINITIONS AND EXPLANATIONS

OF TERMS USED IN

POLITICAL ECONOMY AND COMMERCE.

Advice, information regarding bills or drafts sent *by letter* from one merchant or banker to another.

Annuity, a sum of money to be paid yearly, for a certain number of years, or till a certain person dies. See p. 125.

Apprentice, a young person bound by indenture or written contract, to serve some individual or company for a certain time, in order to be instructed in some art or trade. See p. 82.

Balance of Trade, the difference between the value of the exports and imports of a country. See p. 115.

Bank, an establishment for the safe keeping of money, to facilitate payments by one to another, and sometimes to grant public loans.

Bank Notes, a banker's promise to pay money. See p. 118.

Bankrupt, a merchant who cannot pay his debts, and who has done one or other of certain acts which the law defines to be acts of bankruptcy.

Barter, exchange of goods for goods. See p. 14.

Bill of Exchange. See "Exchange," and p. 115.

Bill of Lading, a formal receipt for goods from the master of a ship, binding himself as a carrier to deliver them to the proper individual.

Bonding Houses. See "Warehousing System," and p. 106.

Bounty, a payment made by government to the producers, or exporters, or importers of certain kinds of goods, or to those who employ ships in certain trades.

Brokers, persons employed as intermediaries between different merchants.

Brokerage, the payment or per centage paid to brokers on the sale or purchase of goods or bills.

Capital. See p. 39. Fixed and circulating. See p. 41.

Cash Account, or Cash Credits. See p. 122.

DEFINITIONS OF TERMS.   159

Check, Cheque, or Draft. See p. 117.

Clearing, a method adopted by London bankers of exchanging the drafts on each others' banks, and settling the differences. See p. 117.

Commerce, a term formed from two Latin words, *commutatio mercium*, which mean exchange of goods.

Commodities. See p. 61.

Communism. See p. 73.

Company, Joint Stock, a company having a certain amount of capital divided into transferable shares, and managed for the common benefit of the shareholders by a certain number of directors chosen by them. After the stock has been subscribed no one can enter such a company without first buying one or more shares from some of the existing members.

Competition. See p. 85.

Consul, an officer sent by the government of one country to reside in another, and to aid the commerce carried on where he resides by the subjects of the country which sends him.

Co-operation. See p. 98.

Copyright, the right which authors and artists claim to the privilege of publishing and selling their works. See p. 112.

Corn Laws, laws imposing duties on imported corn. See p. 108.

Cost of Production. See p. 22.

Credit. See p. 113.

Currency. See p. 121.

Customs, duties or taxes charged on goods which are imported into or exported from a country. See p. 105.

Discount, a payment made on account of the immediate advance of money not due till some future period. See p. 53.

Dividend, the payment made to creditors from the estate of a bankrupt, and to those who receive interest from public funds.

Docks, artificial basins in which ships can lie, or be repaired.

Dock Warrants, written orders from the authorities at the docks by means of which importers receive their goods.

Exchange, a term sometimes limited to mean transactions by means of which the debts of those who reside in different countries from their creditors can be paid without actual sending of money. See p. 115.

Excise, taxes on goods produced and consumed at home. See p. 105.

Funds, the public debt of the Government. See p. 48.

Incidence of Taxation. See p. 106.

Insurance, or Assurance, a contract by which one party engages for a certain payment to insure another against any risk to which he may be exposed.

Interest. See p. 47.

Letter of Credit, a letter written by one merchant or banker to another, requesting him to credit the bearer with a certain sum of money. See p. 116.

Licences, permissions to engage in certain businesses, as pawnbrokers, auctioneers, and the like.
Lock-outs. Se p. 95.
Margin of Cultivation. See p. 79.
Metayer System. See p. 79.
Money, coins, or other things of definite value, which represent the value of all other goods, and by means of which these can be conveniently exchanged. See p. 14.
Monopoly, a grant to some one individual or company of the sole right of selling, making, importing, or exporting certain kinds of goods.
Navigation Laws, laws which formerly existed preventing the importation of goods from Asia, Africa, or America into Great Britain except in English ships; and of goods from any country in Europe except in British ships, or ships which were the property of the people of the country in which the goods were produced. These laws gave a monopoly of the carrying trade in foreign goods to English shipowners.
Patent. See p. 111.
Permit, a licence or paper granted by the officers of excise to remove goods subject to excise duties.
Price. See p. 65.
Rent. See p. 76.
Smuggling, the cheating of the revenue by bringing in foreign goods without payment of the duties; or by selling home-made goods liable to excise duties without payment of the duties. See p. 111.
Socialism. See p. 73.
Speculators. See p. 49.
Standard of Value, single and double. See p. 19.
Stores, Bonded. See "Warehousing System," and p. 106.
Strikes. See p. 92.
Tariff, a table of the duties charged upon importation and exportation of goods.
Taxes. See p. 103.
Truck System, a mode of paying the wages of workmen in goods instead of money.
Usury, very high interest. See p. 54.
Value. See p. 14.
Warehousing System, the mode of providing for the keeping of imported goods in public warehouses or stores, called bonding houses, at a reasonable rent, without payment of the duties on importation till the goods be withdrawn for consumption. See p. 106.
Wages. See p. 23.

William Collins, Sons, & Co.'s Educational Works.

COLLINS' SERIES OF FIRST-CLASS SCHOOL ATLASES,

Carefully Constructed and Engraved from the best and latest Authorities, and Beautifully Printed in Colours, on Superfine Cream Wove Paper.

MODERN GEOGRAPHY—Crown Series.

	s.	d.
MY FIRST ATLAS, consisting of 12 Maps, 9 inches by 7½ inches, folded 8vo, in Neat Wrapper, ...	0	6
THE PRIMARY ATLAS, consisting of 16 Maps, 9 inches by 7½ inches, 4to, Stiff Wrapper, ...	0	6
THE POCKET ATLAS, consisting of 16 Maps, folded in 8vo, and mounted on Guards, cloth lettered, ...	1	0
THE JUNIOR, OR YOUNG CHILD'S ATLAS, consisting of 16 Maps, 4to, with 16 pp. of Questions on the Maps, in Neat Wrapper,	1	0
THE STANDARD SCHOOL ATLAS, consisting of 24 Maps, Crown 4to, in Neat Wrapper, ...	1	0
THE PROGRESSIVE ATLAS, consisting of 32 Maps, 9 inches by 7½ inches, 4to, cloth lettered, ...	2	0
THE CROWN ATLAS, consisting of 32 Maps, on Guards, with Index, 8vo, cloth lettered, ...	2	6
THE NATIONAL ATLAS, consisting of 32 Maps, 4to, with a Copious Index, cloth lettered, ...	2	6

MODERN GEOGRAPHY—Imperial Series.

	s.	d.
THE SELECTED ATLAS, consisting of 16 Maps, Imperial 4to, 11 by 13 inches, Stiff Cover, ...	1	6
THE PORTABLE ATLAS, consisting of 16 Maps, folded Imperial 8vo, cloth lettered, ...	2	0
THE ADVANCED ATLAS, consisting of 32 Maps, Imperial 4to, cloth lettered, ...	3	6
THE ACADEMIC ATLAS, consisting of 32 Maps, Imperial 4to, with a Copious Index, cloth lettered, ...	5	0
THE STUDENT'S ATLAS, consisting of 32 Maps, and 6 Ancient Maps, with a Copious Index, Imperial 8vo, cloth lettered, ...	6	0
THE COLLEGIATE ATLAS, consisting of 32 Modern, 16 Historical, and 2 Ancient Maps, mounted on Guards, with a Copious Index, Imperial 8vo, cloth lettered, ...	7	6
THE INTERNATIONAL ATLAS, consisting of 32 Modern, 16 Historical, and 14 Maps of Classical Geography, with Descriptive Letterpress on Historical Geography, by W. F. Collier, LL.D.; and on Classical Geography, by L. Schmitz, LL.D., with Copious Indices, Imperial 8vo, Cloth mounted on Guards, ...	10	6

PHYSICAL GEOGRAPHY—Demy Series.

	s.	d.
THE PRIMARY ATLAS OF PHYSICAL GEOGRAPHY, 16 Maps, Demy 4to, 9 by 11 inches, Stiff Cover, ...	1	0
THE POCKET ATLAS OF PHYSICAL GEOGRAPHY, 16 Maps, on Guards, Demy 8vo, cloth, ...	2	0

London, Edinburgh, and Herriot Hill Works, Glasgow.

William Collins, Sons,

COLLINS' SERIES OF SCHOOL ATLASES

PHYSICAL GEOGRAPHY—Imperial Series. *s. d.*
THE PORTABLE ATLAS OF PHYSICAL GEOGRAPHY, 20 Maps, 11 by 13 inches, mounted on Guards, Imp. 8vo, cloth, ... **3 6**
THE STUDENT'S ATLAS OF PHYSICAL GEOGRAPHY, 20 Maps, mounted on Guards. With Letterpress Description and Wood Engravings. By James Bryce, LL.D., F.R.G.S. Imp. 8vo, cl., **5 0**

HISTORICAL GEOGRAPHY.
THE POCKET ATLAS OF HISTORICAL GEOGRAPHY, 16 Maps, 6½ by 11 inches, mounted on Guards, Imperial 16mo, cloth, **1 6**
THE CROWN ATLAS OF HISTORICAL GEOGRAPHY, 16 Maps, with Letterpress Description by Wm. F. Collier, LL.D., Imperial 16mo, cloth, ... **2 6**
THE STUDENT'S ATLAS OF HISTORICAL GEOGRAPHY, 16 Maps, Letterpress Description by Wm. F. Collier, LL.D., 8vo, cloth, **3 0**

CLASSICAL GEOGRAPHY.
THE POCKET ATLAS OF CLASSICAL GEOGRAPHY, 15 Maps, Imperial 16mo, 6½ by 11 inches, cloth lettered, ... **1 6**
THE CROWN ATLAS OF CLASSICAL GEOGRAPHY, 15 Maps, with Descriptive Letterpress, by Leonhard Schmitz, LL.D., Imperial 16mo, cloth lettered, ... **2 6**
THE STUDENT'S ATLAS OF CLASSICAL GEOGRAPHY, 15 Maps, Imperial 8vo, with Descriptive Letterpress, by Leonhard Schmitz, LL.D., cloth lettered, ... **3 0**

SCRIPTURE GEOGRAPHY.
THE ATLAS OF SCRIPTURE GEOGRAPHY, 16 Maps, with Questions on each Map, Stiff Cover, ... **1 0**
THE POCKET ATLAS OF SCRIPTURE GEOGRAPHY, 16 Maps, 7½ by 9 inches, mounted on Guards, Imp. 16mo, cloth, ... **1 0**

BLANK PROJECTIONS AND OUTLINES.
THE CROWN ATLAS OF BLANK PROJECTIONS, consisting of 16 Maps, Demy 4to, on Stout Drawing Paper, Stiff Wrapper, ... **0 6**
THE CROWN OUTLINE ATLAS, 16 Maps, Demy 4to, Stout Drawing Paper, Stiff Wrapper, ... **0 6**
THE IMPERIAL ATLAS OF BLANK PROJECTIONS, consisting of 16 Maps, Imperial 4to, on Stout Drawing Paper, Stiff Wrapper, **1 6**
THE IMPERIAL OUTLINE ATLAS, 16 Maps, Imperial 4to, Stout Drawing Paper, Stiff Cover, ... **1 6**

London, Edinburgh, and Herriot Hill Works, Glasgow.

www.ingramcontent.com/pod-product-compliance
Lightning Source LLC
Chambersburg PA
CBHW031455160426
43195CB00010BB/984